Ralph Gardiner

Englands Grievance Discovered in Relation to the Coal Trade

With the Map of the River of Tine, and Situation of the Town and Corporation of

Newcastle

Ralph Gardiner

Englands Grievance Discovered in Relation to the Coal Trade
With the Map of the River of Tine, and Situation of the Town and Corporation of Newcastle

ISBN/EAN: 9783337064020

Printed in Europe, USA, Canada, Australia, Japan

Cover: Foto ©Suzi / pixelio.de

More available books at **www.hansebooks.com**

GRIEVANCE DISCOVERED,

IN RELATION TO THE

COAL TRADE;

WITH THE

MAP OF THE RIVER OF TINE, AND SITUATION OF THE
TOWN AND CORPORATION

OF

NEWCASTLE:

THE TYRANNICAL OPPRESSION OF THOSE MAGISTRATES,
THEIR CHARTERS AND GRANTS; THE SEVERAL
TRYALS, DEPOSITIONS, AND JUDGEMENTS
OBTAINED AGAINST THEM;

WITH A BREVIATE OF SEVERAL STATUTES PROVING REPUGNANT TO
THEIR ACTINGS; WITH PROPOSALS FOR REDUCING THE EXCESSIVE
RATES OF COALS FOR THE FUTURE; AND THE RISE OF
THEIR GRANTS APPEARING IN THIS BOOK.

By RALPH GARDINER,
OF CHIRTON, IN THE COUNTY OF NORTHUMBERLAND, GENT.

LONDON:

PRINTED FOR R. IBBITSON, IN SMITHFIELD, AND
P. STENT, AT THE WHITE HORSE, IN GILTSPUR
STREET, WITHOUT NEWGATE, 1655.

NEWCASTLE:

REPRINTED BY D. AKENHEAD AND SONS, FRONTING
THE EXCHANGE, 1796.

EDITORS' ADDRESS.

WHEN we view the numerous improvements made, within the space of a few years, in many harbours of this kingdom, by the spirited exertions of individuals, and the amazing increase of the towns of these respective ports, in wealth and magnitude, the mind is forcibly impressed with an high sense of the great advantages derived therefrom.

The extensive coal-mines of this country have caused this port always to be considered of the first consequence; not only on account of a great part of the kingdom being supplied therefrom with that necessary article, but for the immense number of ships, necessarily employed, being the first nursery for seamen in the island; and when we reflect that the increasing trade and affluence of this town and port, depend so much upon the preservation of the river, the serious attention of all concerned therein, ought certainly at all times to be directed to every improvement it is capable of receiving.

The design of the liberal author of the following ingenious work, hath been, it evidently appears, to evince the utility of such improvements in this country;

country; as well as to remove many exifting grievances of that period; on which important fubjects, no one has more eminently diftinguifhed himfelf.

After fome degree of difficulty in our fearch for it, we have been favoured with an original copy; and being repeatedly folicited thereto, by a number of refpectable gentlemen, have reprinted the whole *verbatim*, with exact *fac fimiles* of the author's map of the river, and curious prints, together with portraits of the refpective kings and queens, &c. and now offer it to the public on as reafonable terms as the nature of fuch chargeable undertakings will admit of.

Newcaftle, Oct. 29, 1796.

FOR

FOR HIS HIGHNESS

OLIVER, LORD PROTECTOR

OF THE COMMONWEALTH OF ENGLAND, SCOTLAND, AND IRELAND, &c.

MAY IT PLEASE YOUR HIGHNESS,

THE nation, finding your fatherly care over them, in the well ordering, and governing, according to the laws, ftatutes, and cuftoms; endeavoring peace, caufing juftice and law to be equally adminiftred, have caufe, and do blefs God for the fame.

Upon ferious confideration whereof, I fhall not dare, or prefume to ufe arguments, to induce your highnefs, to lend an ear, to hear the nations grievance, or what may be prefented for its good; but do humbly prefent herein, fome collections of records, taken out of moft judicatures, concerning the abufe of the coal-trade, the burrough, and corporation of Newcaftle upon Tine, its charters, evidences, and depofitions; proving thereby general wrongs, and infupportable burdens, viz.

Firft, forcing people to lofe their lives, others to fwear againft themfelves, others to cut purfes in their courts for gain, and all to themfelves; illegal and

and falfe arrefts, and imprifonments; refufers of bail, and difobeyers of *habeas corpufes*; great and ufual impofitions, and arbitrary fines; contemners of your law; judges, jurors, and witneffes in their own caufes; converting all fines, felons goods, and wrecks, to their own ufe; deftroyers of that famous river of Tine; forcing fhips and boats to fink, and imprifoning thofe that dare to fuccor them; ingroffers of all coals, and other commodities, into their own hands, from the inheritors, by patent; with other irrefiftable oppreffions, like to the Spanifh inquifition, and practice of the high commiffion, and ftar-chamber; being put in execution, at this day, in that town, by command of the magiftrates, and other their officers; and what they cannot do, by force of their charter, amongft themfelves, againft any private perfon oppofing, then, by combination, ruin them at law, by their delatory plea, and out-purfing them; to the high difhonor of God, and your highnefs, and tending to the peoples undoing.

Humbly befeeches, for the glory of God, the fame of your law, the contentment of the free people of England, the prefervation of trade and navigation, and increafe of your public revenue,

II. That no confirmation bee of that towne of Newcaftle upon Tines charters, or ufurped powers; but that a fpeedy remedy be had, either by *quo warranto*, or otherwife; and their magiftrates may fuffer, according to their offences.

III. That no arrefts be made in that town, except by procefs from above, or under forty fhillings; by reafon they underftand not the law, and commonly their judges will mafter reafon.

IV. That

IV. That commiffioners of fewers in Northumberland, and county of Durham, be forthwith impowred, for the prefervation of that river; otherwife it will be quite choaked up, and thereby no coals to be got, but at exceflive rates.

V. That an *ad quod damnum* be granted, for a market at Shields, which will prevent the lofs of many a poor fouls life for the future.

VI. Or that a revival of that never to be forgotten ftatute, 11 Rich. 2. cap. 7. for a free trade to all, which voided all monopolies and charters, as being the greateft grievance in a commonwealth, &c. It will not onely make this your nation equivalent with Venice, Holland, and other free rich ftates, in riches, but preferve timber, and reduce coals under 20s. the chalder all the year at London, but alfo augment to your publique revenue above 40000l. per ann. in that very port of the river of Tine.

VII. That your royal protection be granted to fuch who profecute a caufe in behalf of your highnefs, from the hand of violence, during the time of their profecution. That the claufe in the 21. k. James, chap. 3. viz. for all informations upon penal ftatutes to be profecuted in the refpective counties, be voyd; by reafon the judges, *alias* fheriffs, are the offenders, and no right can be got againft them; the honorable judges of both benches hands being tyed up, for want of an appeal, obftructed by the aforefaid ftatute.

VIII. If their charters, and illegal privileges be confirmed, undoubtedly it will facrifice the peace of your nation, leffen your intereft with the free-born, weaken your power, loofe the bonds of a quiet government,

government, extirpate the pure laws, and advance diforder and confufion; it being humbly conceived this happy change of government voids their charters, (they being no laws, but merely prerogatives) to Englands comfort.

IX. That fheriffs and their fubftitutes may be liable to the punifhment of perjury, for breach of their oath, in denying bail to fuch as are capable; for not returning writs of *habeas corpus*, and other their falfe returns, as others in other natures.

X. And that a law be created for death, to fuch that fhall commit perjury, forgery, or accept of bribery.

XI. All which are laid at your highnefs and councils feet, to do as God fhall direct, for the relief of the oppreffed.

Ever fubfcribing myfelf,

A fervant to your highnefs,

And the publique,

RALPH GARDINER.

TO THE READER.

COURTEOUS READER,

I SET not out the map of the river of Tine, for ships to steer their course by; but for a demonstration to such judges as may be appointed regulators of the great abuses done thereunto; nor the effigies in my book, for other corporations to act the like by; but that the irregular proceedings therein, and cruelty of this corporation of Newcastle, may the plainer appear; not onely to his highness, and council, parlament, admiral, army, judges, gentry, but also to the commonalty of the nation; that they may expel out of their thoughts such tyranny as is there enacted, by charter law; being nothing more of my labours and pains than what I am bound in duty, and conscience, for the relief of the oppressed; resolving with Gods assistance to continue so doing, to the uttermost of my power. Probably I may have omitted some circumstances relating, yet am I confident nothing comprehended but the naked truth; and what omissions are in this, in my next will appear, (if I miscarry not, by an unknown hand). I doubt not but some person, may answer this in print, or require further satisfaction therein; I am ready to receive the one, and declare the other; but well I know, the truth hereof cannot be disproved; such may (if they please) whose natural dialect is detraction, apt to stain and sting with calumny and slander, sooner than make a just defence, to joyn issue upon, to stand and fall by (as I am by this) challenging any to brand me with the least of injustice I ever did them; being ready with my fortune to make good what I prosecute. The thing I aim at, is a right understanding between the free and unfree men of England; a perfect love, every one injoying their own, and

THE EPISTLE TO THE READER.

to be governed under our known and wholesome laws, as also an obedience thereunto; and not by a hidden prerogative, alias charters.

It being a wonder there dare be such presumption in this corporation, to exercise such insolencies, which were the greatest obstructors of our nations liberties, by garisoning that town. The mayor, aldermen, and recorder, with the burgesses, and others, against the free-born of England, which prohibited all trade, from the 9th. day of January, 1642, to the 14th of November, 1644, in that port; which caused coals to be four pound the chaldron, and salt four pound the weigh; the poor inhabitants forced to flie the country, others to quarter all armies upon free quarter; heavy taxes to them all, both English, Scots, and garisons; plundered of all they had; land lying waste; coal-pits drowned; salt-works broken down; hay and corn burnt; town pulled down; mens wives carried away, by the unsatiable Scots, and abused; all being occasioned by that corporations disaffection; and yet to tyrannize, as is hereafter mentioned; I appeal to God and the world.

RALPH GARDNER.

CHARTER

JOHN.

PRACTICE DISCOVERED.

CHAP. I.

NEWCASTLE UPON TYNES PATRON.

KING JOHN,

Surnamed without land, raigned 17 yeers and 7 monthes, died 19. daie of October, 1216, was buried at Worcefter, in the 51. yeer of his age.

(A) KING JOHN, who ufurped the crown of England, was (only for formalities fake) fworn by a bifhop, who being demanded the reafon why he did fo, faid, that by the gift of prophecy, certified, that at fome time, king John would take the crown and realm of England, and bring all to ruin and confufion, he pretending, the king his brother, was dead in the time of his being abfent beyond fea; being the firft author of charters (for gain) and people like himfelf, for lucre of gain, fold their birth-right to become bodies corporate, and oppreffors of the free-born people of England: For before charters were, all the free-holders of England were free to make laws for the good of the nation; but corporations being subordinate to such laws, as he by his prerogative gave them, being repugnant to the known fundamental laws of England.

In the first year of his reign, dreadful tempestuous weathers by rains, that the grounds were so spoiled, that whereas corn was sold for one shilling the boule, in king Henry the seconds daies, then cost 13 shillings the boule; also an abundance of fish found dead upon the land, by the corruption of the waters, no hay could be mowed, and hale as big as hens eggs.

(B) He was an usurper, a tyrant, a bloody person, a murderer, a perjured person, a covetous person, a demolisher of famous towns with fire, and a seller of Englands supremacy to the pope*, whose reign was oppressive, and end, shame. For further satisfaction I refer you to his true history, I shall onely give a brief of some passages in his reign.

He made a law that all jews that would not turn christians should pay a certain great sum of money, or be imprisoned, and when they did turn, then they should have their money again; a young merchant paid 60l. to continue a jew, and after turned to be a christian; then he demanded his money from the king, but he being unwilling to part with money, demanded what reason he had to turn, and sent for his father and mother to dif-swade him, and to per-swade him to change again to be a jew.

(C) He gave command that all the jews in England and Wales to be forthwith imprisoned, men, women, and children, by reason they turned so fast to be of his religion, and then seized on all their riches to satisfie his covetous disposition, and such as would not confess where their money was, pulled out their teeth and eies, and then took the thirteenth part of all estates moveable, to war against the earls of Marsh, who desired him to forbear, but he would not, for which they dispossessed him of all his lands in France, &c.

He

* See chap. 49. (B)

He having little love to his wife Ifabel the queen, was divorced, pretending fhe was too near of kin to him, and fo took another.

(D) He murthered duke Arthur earl of Brittan, his eldeft brothers fon, being heir to the crown, in the caftle of Roan, in France, and chafed William de Branes out of England, and caufed his wife and children to be ftarved to death, in Winfor caftle.

He dif-inherited many of the nobility without judgment of the law, and put to death Ramp earl of Chefter, for reproving him for lying with his brothers wife, and reproached others of his nobles, telling them how often he had defiled their beds, and defloured their daughters.

(E) He granted to the city of London their charter, and letters pattents, to chufe their mayor yeerly in the tenth yeer, 1210. who governs well, &c.

(F) He removed the exchequer from London to Northampton, and got a great army to go againft the king of Scots, but the king of Scots met him and did him homage, and gave him his two daughters as pledges, and eleven thoufand fcotch marks, and upon his return took homage of the free-holders of England, and fware them to his allegiance, all above 11 years of age.   11 year 1211.

(G) He made oath to be obedient to the pope of Rome, by name Innocentius, to Randolph, his bull, who went with his nobles to Dover, where he met with the faid popes bull, and there refigned 13 year 1212. the crown with the realm of England and Ireland into the popes hand; fee his oath in chap. 59. (B): upon which the bifhops who he had banifhed, returned to England, by leave from the pope. King John met them and fell flat upon his face on the ground, and afked them forgivenefs, melting bitterly into tears, &c.

(H) He grants the very next year, after his power was given to the pope, unto the town of Newcaftle upon Tyne, letters pattents to be a corporation, and

to

to hold the said town in fee-farm, at the rent of 100l. per. annum, as by the said recited letters pattents, in the second chapter, more at large appears,

14 year, 1213 — anno 1213. (Surely this charter is not good by law, &c.)

(I) He was the cause of firing the chief town in Northumberland, called Morpeth, and caused many more towns in England and Wales to be burnt.

The barons of England being armed, demanded of him the laws and liberties granted by king Edward the confessor, vulgarly called St. Edward, he desired respite till easter, and gave sureties to perform them.

15 year. — (K) He met with the barons of England in Running Meadow, between Winsor and Stains, upon the 16. of June; granted under his hand to them the liberties of England, without any difficulty, and the whole realm was sworn thereunto; and soon after subtlely and privately sends to the pope and other nations, for armies to make void those charters and liberties granted to the barons, and to subdue England, and promised them great rewards. Forty thousand souldiers, that were to have Norfolk and Suffolk, to conquer England for king John, were all cast away on the sea. The pope sends in great strength, who landed at Dover, and destroyed many towns by fire, and with the sword slew many thousands of people; the pope excommunicating the barons particularly by their names great subversion and dissolution thereupon fell, laying all hedges and ditches level, tormenting the barons, with their wives, &c.

16 year. — (L.) The barons were necessitated to send for Lewis, son to the king of France, for to come with an army to join with them to conquer king John, whose cruelties were intollerable; which was done, and king John overthrown, and forced to flee towards Lin; being poysoned by a monk at Swinsted: (The reason he gave was, that if he had lived
half

half a year longer, a half-penny loaf would coft
20s.) He died, and was buried at Worcefter, and 17 year.
king Henry the third, fon to king John, of nine
years of age, was crowned at Glocefter, &c.

(M) The reafon of king John his granting charters
in England, and making corporations, was, for that
he had but little land, to raife great rents from them,
and to affift him with ftrength by out-voting the
knights of (M) the fhires, as is hereafter expreft: For
all free-holders of England that had forty fhillings a
year, met two times a yeer at Seffions Meadows, neer
Rockingham Caftle, in Northampton-fhire, and
there made fuch laws as the nation was governed by,
and confirmed by the king.

(N) King John refolving to have monies and aid
of men, to go to Normandy, to conquer them, could
not conveniently motion it, by reafon of the nume-
roufneffe of the free-holders, but made a fpeech to
them, that he had contrived a very fit and convenient
way, for the making laws for the good of the whole
nation, which was, that by reafon he conceived it a
great trouble, for all them to come fo far for that
purpofe, onely to make laws, that they would chufe
two knights of every fhire and county, in England
and Wales, and give to them the full power of the
nation, and then the faid knights to come and fit with
him in parliament, at Weftminfter, and alfo to allow
them four fhillings a day, out of the county ftock,
which more plainly appears in the ftatute of 35. Hen.
8. ch. 11. Knights to have 4s. per diem, and burgeffes 2s. per diem.

(O) King John when he had got the hundred and
four knights in parliament, they having the full power of the nation from the free-holders, immediately required from them, great fubfidies, and armies to go
for Normandy, to recover fuch lands as he had loft.

(P) The knights anfwered, they onely were intrufted to make laws, and not to taxe the free-holders,
who had intrufted them, and not to raife armies, and

that

that by so doing, they could not discharge the trust reposed in them.

(Q.) The king finding his expectation frustrated, having nothing doubted, but to have wrought his design on so small a number, mastered his passion, and not long after acquainted the knights, that he was sorry for the great burden which lay upon them for making laws, being for a publick, and that they were too few in number, and that he had found out a way how to ease them, and bring in a great revenew to free the nation from impositions.

(R) Which was, that he resolved to incorporate all the great towns in England and Wales, and depute magistrates, to govern as his lieutenants, and every corporation should hold their town in fee-farm, from him and his heirs at a certain rent, some more, others lesse, according to the quality, &c.

(s) Also that every corporation should chuse two burgesses to sit and vote with them, in parliament, they knowing the state of every county. and the burgesses of the corporation (by which means, the burgesses being more in number than the knights might out-vote them, and vote for him) the knights medled not therein at all, but were out-voted by these vassals and tenants to the king, they granting to him whatever he demanded, or else must forfeit their charters: And he granted to them whatever they demanded, &c.

(T) The free-holders of England were represented in parliament, by their knights in their election: And if the burgesses were free-holders, then represented in the same knights.

(v) But if the burgesses were no free-holders then no power in England to make laws, or to sit in parliament, to out-vote the true representative, which are the knights, especially representing no body further then the will of the king, who was onely to confirm laws, but not to make them.

King John had four considerations in making great towns corporations:

1 To

1. To affume a prerogative.
2. To raife vaft fums of mony.
3. To divide the nation.
4. To enflave bodies corporate, by being his vaffals and flaves.

Charters are no laws, and nothing is binding that is not lawful, no laws are made but by parliament, read ftat. 2. Edw. 3. 8.

CHAP. II.

Newcaftles firſt charter.

(A) KING JOHN, by his letters pattents, dated the   day of   in the fourteenth yeer of his reign, and in the yeer of our Lord, 1213, granted, demifed, and confirmed, to the honeft men of the Newcaftle upon Tyne, and to their heirs, his town of Newcaftle upon Tyne, with all the appurtenances, to fee-farm, for one hundred pounds, to be rendred to the faid king and his heirs, at his Exchequer, (to wit.) at the feaft of eafter, fifty pounds, and at the feaft of St. Michael other fifty pounds; faving to the faid king, the rents prizes, and affizes in the port of the faid town. Further he grants to them, and confirmeth one hundred and ten fhillings and fixpence of rent, which they have by the gift of the faid king, in the faid town, of efcheats, to be divided and affigned to them, who loft their rents by occafion of a ditch or trench, and of the new work made under the caftle, towards the river or water, fo that thereof they might have the more, that loft the more, and they that loft the leffe, fhould have the leffe. He alfo granted to them, for him and his heirs, that in nothing they fhould be anfwerable to the fheriffe, nor to the conftable, for thofe things which belong to them, as the faid charter teftifieth. Wherefore he willeth and firmly commandeth, that the faid men

men, and their heirs, may have and hold the fame town with its appurtenances to fee-farm, for the faid hundred pounds yeerly to be paid, as is aforefaid, well and in peace, freely, quietly, and intirely, with all liberties and free cuftomes, which they were wont to have in the time of king Henry the 2. father of the faid king John, as by the faid letters pattents appeareth. The faid king John was the caufe of burning Morpeth, the chief town in Northumberland, and many more towns in Wales, becaufe of the enmity between him and the family of the Bruces, who originally were planted in Wales. Wherefore the faid charter made by the faid king John, to the faid honeft men of Newcaftle upon Tyne, cannot be valid in law, becaufe in the fourteenth yeer of his reign, he fubjected himfelf to be a vaffal to the pope of Rome, as is aforefaid, and for many other reafons mentioned in the faid charter itfelf, confidered in themfelves.

In this charter of king John, that he grants to the honeft men of Newcaftle upon Tyne, he mentions not the port of the river of Tyne, from Sparhawk, at Tynemouth-bar, upon the fea, to Hadwyn-ftreams, above Newburn, in Northumberland; neither is there fo much as one fyllable, whereby the faid king grants to them the two third parts of the faid river, or any of the fifhing, between the faid places, &c.

CHAP. III.

(A) **KING** Henry the third being earneftly fupplicated by the good men of Newcaftle, to confirm king Johns charter, which was done upon the fecond day of July, in the year of our Lord, 1234. the faid king Henry did not inlarge their jurifdiction at all, but onely grants them the charter in the very fame words as king John had in his charter granted.

(B) King

(b) King Henry the third, by his letters pattents, under the great feal of England, dated at Weftminfter, the firft day of December, in the three and twentieth year of his reign, upon the good men of Newcaftles fupplication, thought it fit, to give them licence to dig coals, and ftones, in the common foil of that town, without the walls thereof, in the place called Caftle-field and the Frith ; and from thence to draw and convert them unto their own profit, in aid of their faid fee-farm rent of a 100l. per annum, and the fame, as often as it fhould feem good unto them; the fame to endure during his pleafure; which faid letters pattents were granted upon payment of twenty fhillings into the hamper: Nothing more was given, neither lands, &c. but only to work the coals, during pleafure, for their own ufe.

(c) King Henry the third was petitioned again by the fame honeft men, for fo they were called by king Johns charters (*probi homines* :) That his majefty would be gracioufly pleafed, to give them all the ftone and coals in a place called the Frith, adjoyning to the former, the better to enable them to pay their fee-farm rent, which alfo was granted, paying forty fhillings per annum, into the hamper, upon the eleventh of May, in the one and thirtieth year of his reign. All which coals and ftones, have, do, and will amount to many thoufands of pounds, yet no land, above the faid coals was granted unto them.

CHAP. IV.

(a) KING EDWARD the firft, in the nineteenth yeer of his reign, was fupplicated by the good men of Newcaftle, to grant them a fum of money,

money, and a licence for the building of a wall round the town (on which wall, one of the mayors of Newcaftle was hanged) as by the record of the regiftery appears, That two third parts of the river of Tyne, from Sparhawk to Beadwyn-ftreams were in this kings hands. And for fuch lords as held any fifhings on the fouth-fide of the faid river of Tyne, which went to the mid-ftream, they were meer intruders of one fixt part more then was their own, for whereas they were to have had but one third part, they claimed half.

(B) And that this king gave licence, to build a wall about the town of Newcaftle, and gave mony towards this wall, which was not beftowed.

(C) And that divers purpreffures were then incroached upon, by the good men of the town of Newcaftle, upon the moat of the Newcaftle, built by William Rufus, adjoyning thereunto. And to the end that the then fheriffe of Northumberland might prefent thefe incroachments into the chancery, whereby to difcover their unjuft dealing and intrufion upon the faid moat of the faid caftle, they the faid good men gave to him the faid fheriffe, a gift or bribe of ten marks, that he might not vex them, as by the faid record more at large appears, &c.

CHAP. V.

THE faid king Edward the third, by his letters patrents, dated at Weftminfter, the tenth day of May, in the one and thirtieth yeer of his reign, confirms all former charters, with an addition of his own, that he, for himfelf and his heirs, granted, demifed, and confirmed unto his honeft men

men of the town of the Newcaftle upon Tyne, his town of Newcaftle, before called Mancheſter, with all its appurtenances, for a hundred pound per annum, to be paid to the faid king, and his heirs, &c. Which he the faid king confirms to the faid men, and burgeſſes, and to their heirs for ever. And becauſe, on the behalf of the faid burgeſſes of the faid town, it was humbly fupplicated to the faid king, that whereas the faid moore and lands called Caſtle-fields, and Caſtle-moor, on the north-fide of the faid town of Newcaſtle, from a certain place called Ingler Dike, &c. as the fame are butted and bounded, &c. even to the faid town of New-caſtle, are the lands and foil of the faid town of Newcaſtle belonging to the fame, beyond memory; with all profits coming of the faid lands, moor, and foil, as by an inquifition thereof taken, and re-turned into the chancery appeareth. And albeit the faid burgeſſes, and their predeceſſors from the time they have had the faid town to farm, they have held the faid moor and land, as though it were appertaining to the faid town, and have always hitherto peaceably, and quietly had, and reaped all the profits coming of the faid moor and lands, yet the faid burgeſſes, (now they are turned from honeſt men, to burgeſſes, the next will be to ————) for that there is no mention made of the faid moor and lands (albeit they be of the appurtenances of the faid town) do fear, that they may be impeached afterwards, and for that the faid town, as well by reafon of the laſt peſtilence at that time, as by the hazards of wars, and divers other adverſities, was fo impoveriſhed, and deſtitute of men, that the profits of the faid town fufficed not for the payment of the faid farm, (as they then pretended.) The faid king being willing to provide for their in-dempnity in that behalf, and for him, and his heirs granted, that they and their heirs might have and hold the fame moor and foil, as if it were appertaining

taining to the said town, with all profits out of the same, &c. And that they the said burgesses, and their heirs, in the said moor and lands, may dig, and may have coal, slait, and stone there; and from thence may draw them, and may make their profit of the said coals, slait, and stones, and other profits coming out of the said moor and lands, in aid of the payment of their said fee-farm, without impeachment, &c. As by the said letters patents, (made by the king himself, and his council, and by the fine of forty shillings paid in the hamper) more at large appeareth.

By these last mentioned letters pattents, the burgesses of Newcastle can challenge no title in the said Castle-moor, and Castle-field, because the said letters pattents are contrary in themselves. This is the first claim the said burgesses lay to the Castle-moor, being a quantity of eight hundred and fifty acres of ground, besides pasture for all their kine, and coals for all their fuel, which are gotten upon the said Castle-moor.

CHAP. VI.

KING RICHARD the second, by his charter, dated the ninth day of April, in the first year of his reign, 1378, confirms all the former charters, and grants to the town of Newcastle, the same priviledge as granted before, in diging of coals, slait, and stone, in Castle-field, and Castle-moor, but doth not grant the (land) onely the coals, slait, and stone, for the towns best advantage.

CHAP. VII.

KING Henry the fourth, being humbly petitioned by the burgeſſes of Newcaſtle, that his highneſſe would be gracioufly pleaſed, to divide the town and corporation, from the county of Northumberland, and to grant them a ſheriffe, with more liberties and immunities, which was granted; that the corporation of Newcaſtle ſhall be a diſtinct county of itſelf, diſ-joyned from the county of Northumberland, and not to meddle in the ſaid new county, as by the charter more at large appears, upon record, in the tower of London, 7 Ed. 6. 10. 1. Mary 3.

This was a preparative for the town of Gateshead, &c.

CHAP. VIII.

(A) QUEEN Elizabeth obtained a leaſe from the late biſhop of Durham, dated the 26. of April, in the 24. year of her reign, 1582. of all the whole mannors of Gates-head and Wickham, and all the coal-pits, and coal-mines within the ſaid mannors of Gates-head and Wickham aforeſaid, and in all the common waſts, and parks belonging to the ſaid mannors, at the rent of ninety pounds, per annum, or thereabouts, for ninety nine yeers, which the earle of Leiceſter procured from the ſaid queen, and ſold, or gave the ſame to Sutton of the charter-houſe, who for twelve thouſand pounds, as is reported, ſold the ſame to the mayor and burgeſſes of Newcaſtle*

* It is conceived, that this leafe is void, by reason the corporation forfeited it, being garrisoned againſt the parliament, &c.

caſtle,* but when he underſtood the yearly value, which was worth at leaſt fifty thouſand pounds per annum, atteſted by doctor Cradock, ſome-times archdeacon of Northumberland, deceaſed, this leaſe being called the grand leaſe, was granted to ſir William Readal, and others, for the uſe of the mayor and burgeſſes, and free honeſt men, and expires the 26. of April, which ſhall be in the year of our Lord, 1681. as appears in the 11. chap. (I.) 7. Edw. 6. 10.

CHAP. IX.

(A) QUEEN ELIZABETH requires the great arrear, of two-pence per chaldron, which was granted to king Henry the fifth, as cuſtome, by the parliament, as appears by that ſtatute, chapter the tenth, ninth year, which was neglected to be paid unto the crown, by the mayor and burgeſſes, for many years together, inſomuch as they were not able to pay the ſame, but humbly beſeeched thoſe arrears may be forgiven, by reaſon of their inability: And to grant them a charter to incorporate a new fraternity or brother-hood to be called free * hoſt-men, for the ſelling and vending of all coals to ſhipping; and in conſideration thereof, they would pay to her majeſty, and her ſucceſſors, twelve pence for every chalder, exported from thenceforth, to the free people of this nation. The queen conceiving that twelve-pence upon every chalder would be better for the future, and well paid, would riſe to a greater revenew then the two-pence ſo long in arrear could endamage, which was granted, upon condition ſpecified in that grant, remaining in the exchequer, with many ſeals to it; that they ſhould ſell all coals to maſters of ſhips: At this day the fitters reckon with the

* Chap. 25.

the mafters for fo much a chalder, as eleven fhillings, for fo many as is conceived to be aboard the fhip, and then he goeth with the mafter to reckon, which the faid mafters payes the one fhilling per chalder cuftome, being allowed in his hand, the mafter conceives he doth not pay it further then being left in his hand by the fitter; but if the mafters will look upon that leafe, they will find they are to have the beft coals for ten fhillings, and the worft for nine fhillings the chaldron, at moft, and now they pay eleven fhillings, by which means the one fhilling per chaldron is paid by the mafter, and not by the hoft-man, and fo falls upon the whole nations back. I refer you further to the leafe, for if the mafter buy dear, he muft needs fell dear.

(B) By the fame fallacy they wronged the king of his cuftomes, 9. Hen. 5. 10. which plainly appears in that ftatute, if you pleafe to read it; the fame, they have to cheat the queen and her fucceffors for the twelve-pence per chaldron.

CHAP. X.

(A) QUEEN Elizabeth being humbly intreated, by the mayor, and burgeffes of Newcaftle, that her majefty would be gracioufly pleafed to grant them a charter of liberties, concerning feajurifdiction, and of admiralty in that port (to wit.) between Sparhawk, in the fea, and Hadwyn ftreams, being fourteen miles in length, for the advance of the eftate of that town, which alfo was granted as follows.

(B) The queen by her letters pattents, dated the thirtieth day of Auguft, in the one and thirtieth year of her reign, touching the office of the high admiralty

This statute of 2. Edw. 3. 8. will void this charter by reason it is against right.

miralty of the river of Tyne, and port of Newcastle, grants the reversion to the mayor and burgesses of Newcastle, by reason it was granted under the great seal of England, bearing date the fifth of February, 1522, unto Charles lord Howard of Effingham, amongst other things, in his said pattent, in the office of lord high admiral of England, &c. for life, who out-lived the queen, and dyed, 26. January, in the sixteenth year of king James, the mayor and burgesses pretending they had right thereunto, from king Henry the sixth, which if they had, was extinguished upon the queens grant to the high admiral, &c. and by this grant of hers to Newcastle, she onely grants what is in her to grant, which is onely the reversion after the surrender, forfeiture, or death of the aforesaid lord high admiral, but she dying before the lord high admiral, it is conceived her grant is void. And it was never since confirmed by any other to the said mayor and burgesses; for king James upon the 28. of June, in the sixteenth year of his reign, two dayes after the lord high admiral died. The commission, or letters pattents of the admiralty of England, was conferred upon the duke of Buckingham, so that Newcastle by this change hath but a slender pretence of right to the admiralty of that part of Newcastle.

Newcastles petition.

(c) The said corporation humbly beseecheth her grace, to increase, inrich, inlarge, and establish (as much as in her lay) their authorities and jurisdiction in sea-businesses, with larger priviledges, exemptions, liberties and immunities, and those being called by various names, to establish into a certain body, and reduce and create the name of the incorporation, upon which petition, the queen made the town and corporation of Newcastle, a free town, in these words.

(D) That the burgesses and inhabitants of the said town from henceforward for ever, shall be one body corporated, or body politick, in substance, fact, and name, by name of a mayor and burgesses. And that

by

by that name, they may have perpetual fucceffion. And perfons able in law, capable to have, purchafe. receive, and poffeffe, lands, * tenements, liberties, jurifdictions, franchifes, and heriditaments, of what kind, nature, or form foever they fhall be, to them and their fucceffors in fee and perpetuity; and to affign them over by the name aforefaid. And by the fame name to implead or fue, and be fued, anfwer, or to be anfwered, defend, or be defended in any court of record.

*Newcaftle incorporated. To purchafe lands. See ftat. 15 Rich. 2. 5.

To fue, and be fued by one name. See Edw. 3. 6.

(E) And to have a common feal for their caufes and bufineffes, and to break and change the fame at their pleafure.

(F) Likewife, fhe confirms by the faid charter, to the faid mayor and burgeffes, and their fucceffors, that they onely of the faid town, with its members and appurtenances, and alfo that they may have all the fame cuftomes, liberties, priviledges, franchifes, immunities, exemptions, quittances and jurifdictions, how many, and how much foever hath been granted by former kings, by what name or names foever, or by what pretence they have or do enjoy or claim the fame. To have and to hold, and to be holden of the faid queen, in fee-farm &c.

Confirms all former liberties.

(G) Alfo grants by the faid charter unto the mayor and burgeffes and their fucceffors, full authority, power, and faculty of mittigamus, conftituting, ordaining, making and eftablifhing, from time to time, fuch laws, * inftitute judgments, ordinances and conftitutions, according to their found difcretion, being good, wholefome, and neceffary for the publick good and weal, and common profit, and good rule of the faid town.

* Making laws, fee ftat. 19. 7.

(H) The mayor and burgeffes, have power hereby to inflict punifhments, pains, penalties, and imprifonments* of bodies, (and by fines, or amerciaments, may levy, and have to them, and their fucceffors without calumny or impeachment) requiring all perfons to yeeld obedience to fuch laws,

*To punifh offenders. See ftat. 9. Hen. 3. 29 Commanding &c obedience.

&c. provided those laws, ordinances, institutions, and such like customes, be not repugnant to the laws and statutes of England.

Sparhawk and Headwyn streams their liberties.

(I) Also that the grants, which the said town of Newcastle, and the circuits, precincts, and jurisdictions thereof, to stand as well in breadth, as length, as well by land, as by water, as was accustomed before the memory of man, as they were wont to extend themselves, and in the river of Tyne, from a place called Sparhawk, in the sea, to Headwyn streams, seven miles above Newcastle-bridge. And to pull down all walls, hedges, and blocks, offensive, &c.

Entrance to the office of high admiralty.

(K) And further, by the said letters pattents, the queen doth grant unto the said mayor and burgesses, upon the surrender of the same, letters pattents of the same high admiral of England, by death, forfeiture, surrender, or other means, to become void for ever. And may have and hold within the said town, one court of admiralty of record, every munday throughout the yeer; in which court,

Keeping courts.

the mayor, or recorder to be one: And to begin upon the vacancy of the said office, to hold by plaint, in the same court to be levied, all, and all manner of pleas, suits, plaints, and demands. For which debts, contracts, covenants, trespasses and deceits, matters, and offences whatsoever, to the said court of admiralty belonging, and to hold court of pleas according to the laws and customes of the said court of admiralty of England, and other legal wayes and means; whereby the truth

Punishment. * See stat. 28. Edw. 3. 3.

may the better be known with power of any temporall constraint * or mulct, or any other pain, according to the laws and customes of the said late queens court of admiralty of England, to be compelled, or to do, and administer judgment, the order of law being kept.

Laws of England executed

(L) And likewise she ordains justices of the peace, to conserve the peace in the said town and port, for the

the putting in execution the statutes and ordinances made at Westminster, in the eighteenth year of king Edward the third, concerning forestalling of merchandizes upon the water, or upon the sea. And the thirteenth of Edward the first, the five and fortieth of Edward the third, the thirteenth of Richard the second, and seventh of Henry the fourth, and Henry the sixth, the four and thirtieth of Henry the eighth, and the fifth and sixth of Edward the sixth statutes, at Westminster against regrators, fore-stallers, and ingrocers, to enquire after such offenders against the laws and statutes aforesaid, to hear and determine such like indictments and punishments. *Fore-stalling. See chap 50. A. 49. 5, 48. A.*

(M) That the serjeant at mace, all juries, panels, inquisitions, attachments, precepts, mandates, warrants, judgments, sentences, processes, or other things whatsoever to do, for the dispatching thereof. *Officers to do their duty. See chap. 36, c. d.*

(N) The queen gives further power unto the mayor, to choose all officers in the said court whatsoever, to remove and expell them, as they shall see cause, according to law and equity.

(O) That the mayor, recorder, and aldermen, three, or more of them, whereof the mayor, or recorder to be one of them, may have for every acknowledgment of all and singular such like pleas, plaints, suits, and demands of debts, and other sea-businesses and offences, and also disseizing of all wrecks* at sea or port, happening, and of the death, drowning and viewing of all dead bodies of what persons soever, which in the said town and port, howsoever slain or drowned, or to be slain, drowned, or murthered, or brought to death by any other means. *See chap 30. B. chap. 29. * All acknowledgements wreck, &c. View of dead bodies murthering, drowning.*

(P) Also the custody and conservation of the statutes, the wreck at sea, and of the office of coroners* in the third and fourth year of king Edward the first, and to punish delinquents, according to law. *Wreck. Coroners. * See ch. 48. A. 29. 49. A.*

D 2 (Q.) The

(Q) The mayor of the same town for ever, hath hereby power to receive acknowledgments, for any cause whatsoever, in the admiralty court determinable, and to record and enrole the said recognizance, to release, cancel, lessen, and qualifie, at their pleasure, according to law. Also to demand execution, according to the manner of the said high court of the admiralty of England.

To fine and qualifie. See stat. 25. Edw. 1. 5.

(R) The said queen doth give and grant, by the said letters pattents, unto the said mayor and burgesses, and their successors, all, and singular fines, redemptions, issues, amerciaments, forfeitures, perquisites, and profits whatsoever appearing, happening, coming, assessed, imposed, or taxed, or then after to be upon any by the aforesaid court, for their own proper use and behoof, without any account to the said queen, or her heirs, to be levied so soon as ever it shall be adjudged by them, without any unquietnesse, vexation, or trouble of the said queen, her heirs and successors, justices, or other ministers, or subjects whatsoever.

All fines for their own use is given. See chap. 42. A. 41. A.

(s) Also to have all manner of such like goods and chattels, weiffs, wrecks * of the sea, goods floating or swimming upon the water, and driven to the shoar*, sunk to the bottom, and goods due, to more by proportion, treasure found, felons of themselves, deodands, and other casualties, as well upon as by the sea or shores, and maritine parts, as upon or by the fresh water, howsoever, whensoever, or wheresoever, or in what manner appearing, happening, or coming, which to the admiralty of England doth belong.

* To have all profits and wrecks.
* See c. 30 A. 29. D. Stat. 17. Ed. 2. 11
To have all felons goods, &c. See chap. 53. A. Stat. 17. Ed. 2. 16.
* Royal fishes. Stat. 17. Ed. 2. 11.

(T) And all royal fishes, sturgeons*, whales, porpoyses, dolphins, rigoseres, and grampeses.

(v) That the said queen willed, that the mayor, recorder and aldermen, for the time being, three or more of them, whereof the mayor or recorder to be one from time to time ever hereafter, to be justices at the goal delivery, and to deliver out of prison in the same,

Justices of goal delivery.

fame, committed to the fame goal, for what caufe foever.

(w) That they may erect gallows within the liberty of the faid town, for felons, murtherers, and other malefactors whatfoever, within the town or port, and to commit them to the goal, till they be from thence delivered, by due courfe of law. See chap. 53. (A.) Gallows and to hang them.

(v) All which of her fpecial favour, fhe grants without fine into the hamper. Dated at Weftminfter, the 30. of Auguft, in the 31. year of her reign. It is conceived this is voyd, by reafon granted without any confideration into the hamper.

CHAP. XI.

A brief of the privileges, contained in the charter of liberties, granted by queen Elizabeth, to the mayor and burgeffes of the town of the Newcaftle upon Tyne, the 22th. of March, in the 42th. year of her reign. As followeth.

The twelve companies of Newcaftle be as follow,

CORDWINDERS,	SKINNERS,
BUTCHERS,	CORN-MERCHANTS,
TAYLORS,	TANNERS,
FULLERS,	SADLERS,
DRAPERS,	BAKERS,
MERCERS,	SMITHS.

I finde not BREWERS nor CARPENTERS. Obferv.

(A) THAT the town of Newcaftle is an ancient town, and that they have had laws, jurifdictions, &c. and that the faid town hath fuffered no fmall lofs, by reafon of divers differences, &c. fol. 1. concerning the manner of loading and unloading fea-coals,

coals, at the fame town, fo. 2 whereupon the faid mayor and burgeffes humbly petitioned the faid late queen, for the better maintenance and government of the faid town, that fhe would vouchfafe to amplifie her munificence and favor towards the faid town. fo. 2.

(B) The faid queen, for her and her fucceffors, grants to the faid mayor and burgeffes, and to their fucceffors, that they only of the faid town with its members, fhall have and enjoy, all the cuftoms, liberties, &c. which were granted to their fucceffors, by feveral charters, fo. 3. which the honeft men of the Newcaftle upon Tyne, &c. by pretence of what corporation foever, they held and enjoyed, fo. 4, 5. to have, hold, and enjoy, the faid town, and all cuftoms, &c. fo. 5. to the faid mayor and burgeffes, and their fucceffors, to their ufe for ever, to be holden in fee-farm; rendring the antient fee-farm of 100l. at michaelmas onely, fo. 6. and that they may have all fuch liberties, cuftoms, &c. without the let of any one, &c. fo. 7.

Choyce of the mayor and other officers.
(c) The faid queen granteth, that the mayor, ten aldermen, and fheriff of the faid town, &c. and other four and twenty of the more difcreet and honefter burgeffes of the faid town, &c. may chufe the mayor, and other officers of the faid town, within five daies, after the choyfe and oath taken by the mayor, fo. 7. 8. which faid mayor, and the other twenty four burgeffes, in all thirty fix, fhall be at all times then after, the common council of the faid town; fo. 9. and fhall have power in making laws, &c. fo. 10. for the good government of the faid town, &c. fo. 11. and for the good government of the markets and fairs, within the faid town and limits thereof, &c. and for the declaration by what means the minifters, officers, and artificers of the faid town, and their factors, fervants, and apprentices in their trades, &c. fo. 12. and alfo for their better prefervation, letting and fetting of their lands tenements, &c. And that the mayor, and common council of the faid town,

Power to make laws for themfelves not repugnant to the laws of England. Caftle-moor is without the limits.

QUEEN ELIZABETHS CHARTER. 23

town, or the greater part of them, whereof we will the mayor and fix aldermen, thirteen being, seven to be, &c as often as they shall make such laws, &c. and such pains, punishments, penalties, or imprisonment of bodies, or by fines, &c. fo. 14. upon all delinquents, contrary to such laws, &c. as shall be necessary for keeping, fo. 15. of the said laws, &c. and to have and retain the said fines, &c. to their own use, &c. fo. 16. so that the same laws, &c. be not repugnant to the laws of the kingdom of England*, fo. 17. *To punish offenders against such laws.*

See stat. 19. Hen. 7. 7.

(D) And further, the said late queen granteth, that the election of the mayor, recorder, aldermen, common council and all other officers and ministers, to be chosen, &c. shall in every year be upon monday next, after michaelmas day, fo. 18. honest men and burgesses of the twelve societies, lawfully chosen in the accustomed place, to wit, drapers, mercers, &c. fo. 19. and that they name and present two honest men of every mystery, &c. being twenty four in number, being sworn that they, or the greatest part of them, shall chuse and name the mayor, fo. 21. the 22. 23. 24. 25. 26. 27. leaves, are concerning the chusing of the mayor the sheriff, of two coroners, one clerk of the chamber, who shall administer an oath to the marriners and masters of ships at the port of Newcastle; and in the same manner, and the same day yearly, may name eight other burgesses, &c. fo. 28. to be chamberlains of the same town, and one sword-bearer before the mayor, and eight fo. 29. serjeants of the mace, and one recorder; fo. 31. and there shall be twenty four electors for one year; fo. 31. 32. new election of alderman, dying or being deposed, fo. 33. and the alderman, newly chosen, shall be alderman during life, fo. 34. Officers chosen by the mayor under their common seal, shall be admitted to their places, fo. 35. 36. 37. To fine such as refuse to hold their places upon election, fo. 38. the said fine not to exceed 200 marks, fo. 39. 40. 41. The like for the sheriff, fo. 42. 43. 44. 45. 46.

Election of the mayor, sheriff, and other officers, at what time.

The port belongs to the castle, and not to the town.

Oath to master of ships.

Officers for life.

To fine refusers of offices.

45. 46. or if any officer (save the recorder) die within the year, then to chuse another, fo. 47. 48. 49. And if the recorder die within one year next after his election, or be removed from, or leave his office, &c. then to choose another fit person, learned in the laws, albeit not a burgess, in his place, &c. fo. 49. 50. 51. And if the mayor of the said town be deposed, removed, or die, then to chuse another within twenty daies, &c. fo. 51. 52. The like for the sheriff, &c. fo. 53. 54. William Jennison named first mayor, fo. 55. 56. John Savel one of the barons of the exchequer, first and modern recorder, fo. 57. William Selby, &c. and nine others are made the first and modern aldermen, fo. 58. James Clavering appointed first, and the modern sheriff, &c. fo. 59. the said William Jennison, mayor, and thirty five persons more, are appointed to be the first and modern common councilmen, &c. fo. 60. 61. Matthew Chapman, and Rowland Tempest are appointed to be first, and the modern coroners, &c. fo. 62. George Dent appointed first clerk of the chamber, fo. 62. Francis Burrel and seven others, appointed to be the first and the modern chamberlains of the said town, fo. 63. George Still appointed sword bearer, fo. 63. George Selby, and seven other persons appointed to be the first serjeants at mace, &c. fo. 63.

(E) The said queen, grants to the said mayor and burgesses, and their successors, for ever, that they may hold one court of record, in Guilde-hall, before the mayor, upon munday in every week, through the year, except in the weeks of christmas, easter, and penticost, &c. fo. 65. and another court, upon wednesdaies and fridaies in every week, throughout the year, except in the several weeks aforesaid; and all pleas of debts, covenants, detainer, trespasses, &c. fo. 66. 67. and pleas of court, of pipowder, &c. fo 68. and courts of the upper-bench, justices of the bench, and justices of assize, before the said mayor, fo. 69. 70. And that the mayor and burgesses in the court,

to

The recorder no burgess.

Every officers name.

From the 18. leaf to the 65. leaf, concerning the officers of Newcastle.

To hold courts of record, see chap. 42. c.

to be holden before the mayor, and in the court, to be holden before the sheriff, and their successors, in all and singular suits, &c. may attatch the parties defendants in the same suits, &c. fo. 71. in their lands and goods, and commit them to their prison, called newgate, &c. fo. 72. 73.

The mayor, the ten aldermen, and recorder of the said town, for ever, to be joyntly, and severally keepers of the peace, &c. within the said town, &c. and to chastise and punish malefactors, &c. fo. 73. 74. 75. 76.

And further, that they, the 12, 11, 10, 9, 8, 7, 6, 5, 4, or 3 of them, whereof the mayor to be one, be justices of the said late queen, her heirs and successors, to enquire upon oath, &c. fo. 76. of all murders, &c. forestallers*, regrators, &c. and of all other matters whatsoever done, or committed, &c. fo. 77. 78. 79. so that the keepers of the peace in Northumberland and Durham, do not enter for any matter of peace, &c. to be ended and determined, in the said town of Newcastle, fo. 80.

Conservators of the peace, chap. 37. chap. 36. To enquire of all misdemeas- norstothelaw forestallers, regrators, &c. * See stat. 5. 6. Ed. 6. 15.

(F) The queen grants to the said mayor and burgesses, and their successors, that they may, as often as need shall require, impose, &c. fines*, penalties, taxations, customs, &c. for the publick use of the mayor and burgesses of the said town, to be kept in their common chamber, and to be expended for their publick use, fo. 81. or by their officers, from time to time to be levied, such as before time, were lawfully taxed and imposed, &c. and that the said mayor, &c. may use all the means they can, to levy and gather the same, fo. 82.

Reasonable taxation of fines, &c. for the towns use. *See stat. 25. Ed. 2. 6.

(G) The queens pleasure further was, that the mayor, recorder, and aldermen of the said town, or five, or more of them, whereof the mayor to be one, be justices for gaol deliveries, &c. fo. 83. and that the coroners * of the said town shall deliver all juries, inquisitions, pannel attatchments, &c. and make return of them to the mayor, &c. in all their gaol

*Gaol delive- ries and co- roners, &c. See stat. 3. H. 7 1. 'Town moor is without their liberties, only liberty to get coals.

E

They have no
other liberties
but within the
walls of the
town.
Quere, what
interest they
have in the
port, for it ex-
tends seven
miles above,
and seven
miles below,
the town of
Newcastle,
which is fur-
ther then their
right of inhe-
ritance reach-
eth.
Queen Eliza-
beth her leafe
of the manor
of Gates side
and Wickham
made to W.
Reddel, and
others in truft,
for the mayor
and burgesses
of Newcastle,
for the time
being See stat.
7. Ed. 6. 10.
*The copy
concerning
the stat. of
mort. whe-
ther the leafe
be good or
not. 15. Rich.
2. 5.

gaol deliveries, &c. fo. 84. and do execute the
precepts of the mayor, &c. in such manner, as any
sheriffe of England was accuftomed to do, at the
gaol deliveries, for their several counties; and that
the said mayor, recorder, and aldermen may, fo. 85.
erect gallows within the liberties of the said town,
to hang felons, &c. And that the said mayor, recorder, and aldermen, or five, or more of them,
may take and arreft what felons, theeves, and malefactors soever, within the town and port of Newcastle, and port aforesaid, or the precinct, or liberties of them, are found, &c. and may bring
them to prison there, fo. 86.

(H) The said queen gives licence to William
Reddel, and to six others, and to what subjects, or
subject whatsoever, of the said late queen, her heirs
and successors, assign or assigns, tenants, or farmers,
fo. 87. of the mannor of Gates-fide, and Wickham,
with their appurtenances, in the county of Durham,
by vertue of a leafe to the said queen, made (amongst
others) by Richard, late bishop of Durham, by his
indenture, dated the 26. of April, in the 24. year of
her reign, 1582. for ninety nine years from the
making thereof; and that the said assign or assigns,
tenants, farmers, fo. 88. of the premises so demised,
and their survivors. The said mannors, or lordships of Gates-fide and Wickham, with their appurtenances, may grant and affign, to the said mayor
and burgesses, and to their successors, for the refidue of the years then to come; and to the mayor
and burgesses of the said town, and to their successors, that the said mannors, and lordships of
Gates-fide, fo. 89. and Wickham aforesaid, with
their appurtenances, may have, and hold, during
the refidue of the years then to come, the said queen,
for her, her heirs, and successors, gave special
licence, notwithstanding the statute of mortmain*
or any other statute, &c. fo. 90.

(I) The

(1) The queen pardoneth and releafeth, to the faid mayor, and burgeffes, and to their fucceffors, and to every fubject and fubjects whatfoever, &c. All, and all manner of pains, penalties, forfeitures, and fums of money, and all other charges whatfoever to the faid queen, or to any her progenitors, fo. 91. theretofore forfeited, by vertue of an act of parliament, of king Henry the fifth, at Weftminfter, in the ninth year of his reign, onely publifhed for the affurement of keels, by parliament commiffioners affigned, or by pretence of another act of parliament, begun at Weftminfter, in the one and twentieth year of king Henry the eighth, fo. 92. intituled, An act concerning Newcaftle, and the port there, for the loading or unloading of any merchants goods, within this kingdome, or elfewhere, to be fold from any fhip or fhips, or other veffels, in or at any place or places, within the port and river of Tyne, between Sparhawk, fo. 93. and Hadwyn ftreams, but only at the faid town of Newcaftle, and not elfewhere, under pains and forfeitures, in the faid act, contained and fpecified. And by vertue of another act of parliament, at Weftminfter aforefaid, the three and twentieth of January, in the firft year of the late queen Elizabeth, intituled, An act, limiting the times of expofing upon land-merchandizes, from parts beyond the feas, and concerning cuftomes and fweet wines, and there it was enacted, amongft others, for and concerning, fo. 94. the loading or unloading in, or from any fhip, or other veffel, any goods, wares, or merchandizes, againft the faid act, &c. or to the late queen, due, and forfeited, by vertue of the faid acts, and all the goods, and chattels, lands, and tenements of the faid mayor, and burgeffes, &c. being the aforefaid penalties and forfeitures, &c. fo. 95.

See this act at the rolls, whetherthere be fuch a penalty or not? becaufe the fame is a private act.

Now followeth the charter of the free-hoaſt-men of Newcaſtle.

(K) MOREOVER the queen grants, to the ſaid mayor, and burgeſſes, and to every ſubject, and ſubjects of hers, her heirs, and ſucceſſors, inhabitants, and burgeſſes of the ſaid town, commonly called hoaſt-men, in every ſeaſon fitting, and hours accuſtomed, the cuſtomes and ſubſidies, and other profits, to the ſaid queen, her heirs and ſucceſſors, due to be paid, and to the cuſtomers, and fo. 96. collectors of the ſaid queen and ſucceſſors, agreeing thereupon to be charged or diſcharged, ſhipped or unſhipped, pit-coals, grindſtones, rub-ſtones, and whet-ſtones, near Newcaſtle, &c. ſuch ſhip, veſſel, &c. was of ſuch a capacity, or for any other reaſonable cauſe, that they could not fitly apply to Newcaſtle, that then, in ſuch caſe, the mayor and burgeſſes of the ſaid town, as their ſervants, &c. fo. 97. might and may, load, and unload, ſuch ſhip and ſhips, veſſel, and veſſels, with coals and ſtones aboveſaid, in their port, between Sparhawk and Newcaſtle, being diſtant by eſtimation not above ſeven miles. And further the queen willeth, fo. 98. and commandeth the ſaid mayor and burgeſſes, &c. and their ſucceſſors, and every ſubject and ſubjects of her, her heirs and ſucceſſors, inhabitants of the ſaid town, called hoaſt-men, that they, the ſame ſhips being of ſuch a capacity, that they cannot fitly ſail to the town of Newcaſtle, to charge and diſcharge themſelves, of coals and ſtones, fo. 99. ſo nigh Newcaſtle, as conveniently may be done, without fraud, &c. and that under the pain of one hundred ſhillings, to be levied for the queens uſe, her heirs and ſucceſſors, to be forfeited for every ſhip or veſſel, ſo charged or diſcharged, contrary to the true intention, mentioned in the ſaid letters pattents, and for that the queen

100 ſhillings for every ſhip or veſſel.

queen willeth, that the mayor, burgeſſes, and inhabitants, of the ſaid town, &c. fo. 100. being burgeſſes, may ſerve the queen and her ſucceſſors with more commendable ſervice, and may furniſh the queen, &c. with mariners, more cheerfully in our greateſt wars, as we have heard they have done in times paſt; and for that the ſaid town hath been a faithful fortreſſe, and defence, fighting againſt the rebels in times paſt, and hath behaved itſelf moſt dutifully to us, and to our progenitors, &c. fo. 101. reſiſting the ſaid rebels. The queen therefore giveth and granteth to the mayor, burgeſſes, and their ſucceſſors, all the felons goods, unto themſelves, and of fugitives, convicted and attainted, and of out-lawed perſons, &c. fo. 102.

All felons goods granted.

(L.) And whereas the town of the Newcaſtle upon Tyne, is a town of merchants, a mart or market of great fame, and ſtuffed with a multitude of merchants, dwelling therein, and of others, as well home-bred thither flowing, and there expecting their trade of merchanting, and thereupon it is neceſſary, to order and eſtabliſh, a certain order, within the ſaid town, fo. 103. and the ſpeedy recovery of debts to merchants, &c. due according to the ſtatute of Acton Burnel, &c. The queen granteth, fo. 104. to the mayor and burgeſſes, and their ſucceſſors, that the mayor for the time, for ever thereafter, ſhall have power, together with the clerk, to that end ordained, to take recognizances, according to the form of the ſtatute of Acton Burnel, and of the ſtatute of merchandize, made in parliament, in the time of king Edward the firſt, and that there ſhall be a clerk in the ſame town, which ſhall be called the clerk of the queen, her heirs and ſucceſſors, to take recognizances of debts, according to the ſaid ſtatute, fo. 105. The queen appoints William Jackſon, gentleman, to be her firſt, and then modern clerk, for taking recognizances of debts, within the ſaid town, to enjoy the ſame, during his life, and after his death, the mayor and burgeſſes, &c.

Halam a rebel they took in the 29. year of king Henry 8. he ſided with ſir Th. Moor, to maintain the popiſh religion, this was here great ſervice.

The queen and her heirs, and ſucceſſors are to have their clerk of recogniſances.

fo. 106.

fo. 106. are impowred to prefer to the said office, fo. 107. another of the burgesses of the said town, to be the queens clerk (as before) and to continue, so long as it should please the mayor, &c. fo. 108. And shall have a seal in two peeces, for sealing the said recognizances, and the mayor to have the custody of the greater peece, and the clerk, fo. 109. shall have the custody of the lesser peece of the said seal, &c. so that if a merchant, or any other shall be made a debtor, he may come before the mayor and clerk of recognizances, and before them acknowledge his debt, and day of payment, fo. 110. And the said mayor and clerk, may do and dispatch all other things, which by the statute aforesaid, are requisite, &c. fo. 111. The said clerk is to have such wages, fees, rewards, and emoluments, for the execution of the said office, as any other mayor, of any other town, or city in England, &c. fo. 112. lawfully, and of right, hath or receiveth, &c. fo. 113.

The mayor to have a seal. See chap. 46. A.

(M) The queen granteth by the said charter, to the mayor and burgesses, and to their successors, and to the inhabitants of the said town, that they be quiet and discharged, fo. 113. of toles, passages, poundage. murage, chimage, paunage, lastage, stallage, carriage, picage, tronage, hidage, and wharfage, for their goods and merchandizes, as well by land as by sea, as well in fares as in markets, and all secular customs, over the queens lands, on this side, and beyond the seas, &c. fo. 114.

The town of Newcastle discharged of toles, &c.

The queen further granteth to the said mayor, burgesses and their successors, that they shall have for their publick use, all and singular such like toles, and all other customs, toles, profits, and advantages, in fares and markets, holden and to be holden within the said town, and any other times whatsoever by themselves, fo. 115. to be levied and gathered, and to be expended to, and for the use of the said mayor and burgesses, and their successors, &c. and the

Profits of toles of markets and fares in Newcastle and liberties, to be levied for the use of the mayor. They may take but pay no toles.

the said queen forbiddeth, that any man disturb them, &c. fo. 116.

(N) The said queen also grants to the said mayor and burgesses, and their successors, that no merchant stranger*, from the liberty of the said town of Newcastle, may sell to any merchant stranger, any their merchandizes within the said town (except victuals, and besides in markets and fares, to be holden within the said town, and limits thereof) nor such merchant stranger may buy any merchandizes, (except and besides, as is before excepted,) fo. 117. of any merchant stranger, within the same town and liberty thereof, other than in gross, upon pain and forfeiture* of those merchandizes, to be had and levied, for the publick use of the said mayor and burgesses, fo. 118.

*See 3 Ed. 1. 20. chap. 29. 48. 49. Merchant strangers selling and buying of merchandizes at Newcastle.
*See stat. Rich 2. 7. 14 Rich. 2 9. 5. 6. Edw. 6. 9. See chap. 51. A.
*See chap. 49. D. chap. 51. A.

The queen moreover granteth, that the said mayor and burgesses, and their successors, fo. 118. may have, hold, &c. all such like liberties, customs, franchises, &c. and all other the premises, &c. to the said mayor and burgesses, granted and confirmed, as is before expressed, and that they may injoy, and use them for ever, fully, freely, &c. without impeachment, molestation, &c. fo. 119.

A general confirmation of all liberties, &c.

Further, the queen pardoneth and releaseth, to the said mayor and burgesses, and to their successors, all, and all manner of actions, suits, impeachments by writ of quo warranto,* to be brought or executed against the said mayor, fo. 120. and burgesses and their successors, by the said late queen, &c. or by any of her officers, by reason of any franchize, liberty, &c. by the said mayor and burgesses, or their predecessors, within the said town, and limits thereof, before times challenged or usurped, and that the said mayor, and burgesses shall be quit, and altogether discharged for ever, fo. 121.

*See stat. 30. Edw. 1. A discharge of all former actions to be brought against them by writ of quo warranto It doth not clear since.

The queen further granteth, that every person or persons, who for ever hereafter shall be admitted to be burgesses, &c. shall be admitted by the mayor and

Burgesses to be admitted by the mayor and burgesses.

and burgesses, &c. or by the greater part of them, fo. 122.

^{A new free grammer-schoole to be erected and called by the name of queen Elizabeth her free grammer-schoole.}

(o) Moreover the queen, often considering in her mind, of how much availe it is to the commonwealth of England, to have youth well educated and instructed from their tender years, &c. fo. 123. ordaineth and granteth, that within the said town of Newcastle, and the liberties thereof, that there be erected, and for ever, there be one free-grammer-schoole, which shall be called the free-grammer-schoole, of queen Elizabeth, in Newcastle, and shall consist of one master and schollars, to be instructed in the same, and that they the master and schollars, of the same school, fo. 124. for ever hereafter, shall be one body corporate, in law, fact, and name, by the name of the master, and schollars, of the free-grammer-schoole of queen Elizabeth, in Newcastle upon Tyne, &c. and by that name may have perpetual succession, and shall be in perpetual times to come, fo. 125. persons able and capable in the law, of having, purchasing, &c. lands, tenements, &c. to them and their successors in fee simple, or for term of years, so they exceed not the yearly value of 40l. and so they be not holden of the said queen, her heirs and successors in chief, nor by knights service, &c. fo. 126. 127. 128. and that the mayor, and burgesses of Newcastle, and their successors, or the greater part of them, &c. fo. 129. shall have power, to make an honest, learned and discreet man, to be the first and modern usher in that school, there to continue, during the good pleasure of the mayor and burgesses, &c. fo. 130. and if it happen the master and usher to die, or leave the said school, &c. fo. 131. then they may chuse other men, to be master and usher, &c. fo. 132. 133.

(P) AND whereas the mayor and burgesses of Newcastle, more deeply considering, and weighing, the effect of divers letters pattents, &c. And whereas the said town is an ancient town, and the

QUEEN ELIZABETHS CHARTER.   33

the mayor and burgesses of the same, time out of
mind, fo. 133. of man, they have had a certain guild
or fraternity, commonly called hoaft-men*, for the
difcharging and better difpofing of fea-coals, and pit-
coals, grind-ftones, rub-ftones, and whet-ftones, in
and upon the river and port of Tyne, which guild or
fraternity is granted, or eftablifhed, by none of the
faid letters pattents: Whereupon the faid mayor and
burgeffes, have humbly fupplicated the faid queen,
that in fupply of the faid defects, that we would ex-
hibit our liberality and favor, fo. 134. and that we
would vouchfafe to make, reduce, and create the
faid guild, into a body corporate and politick, &c.
The faid queen therefore ordaineth, fo. 135. appointeth, and granteth, that William Jennifon, the
elder, and 44 perfons more, commonly called the
hoaft-men, of the faid town of Newcaftle upon Tyne,
and brethren of the faid fraternity, and all others,
which now are, or hereafter fhall be elected, admitted, &c. into the faid guild, or fraternity, of
the faid hoaft-men, of Newcaftle upon Tyne, fo.
136. 137. hereafter, and fhall, be one body corporate and politick, in law, fact, and name, by the
name of the governor and ftewards, and brethren
of the fraternity of the hoaft-men, in the town of
Newcaftle upon Tyne, &c. one body corporate
and politick, really and at full, for us, our heirs
and fucceffors. We do erect, make, ordain and
create, &c. and that by the fame name, they may,
and fhall, have a perpetual fucceffion, and are, and
fhall be, in perpetual times to come, perfons able,
and in law capable, to have, purchafe, receive, and
poffefs, fo. 138. lands, tenements, liberties, &c.
to them and their fucceffors, in perpetuity,* and
otherwaies, and to give, grant, demife, &c. the
fame lands, tenements, and hereditaments, and
to do all other things, by the name aforefaid, and
that by the fame name, they may plead, or be im-
                F   pleaded,

* See ftat. 21.
Jacobi cap. 3.
Mayor and
burgeffes peti-
tion, having
been an anti-
ent fraternity
commonly
called hoaft-
men, for the
difcharging
and better dif-
pofing of fea-
coals, &c. that
they may be
incorporated
in one body.
The queen or-
daineth them
fo to be.
Names 45 to
be the guild
or body cor-
porate.
This is called
a monopoly,
in the ftat. of
the 21. k.
Jam. c. 3.

Enables them
to become
purchafers in
perpetuity.
* See ftat. 15.
Rich. 2. 5. 7.
Ed. 1.

pleaded, &c. in what court foever, &c. fo. 139. 140.

To make a seal, and break it at pleasure. See chap. 46. (A.)

(Q) And that the said governor, and stewards, and brethren, of the hoast-men of the town, fo. 140. of Newcastle, aforesaid, and their successors, that seal at their pleasure, may break, alter, and make, as to them shall seem good. And the queen appointeth, that there be and shall be for ever hereafter, of the number of the hoast-men, &c. which yearly upon the fourth of Jan. fo. 141. shall be chosen, &c. by the said brethren of that fraternity, &c. to be governor, &c. And likewise there shall be, for ever hereafter, two honest and discreet men, of the said number of hoast-men, &c. fo. 142. who shall be the said fourth of January, chosen by the said governor, steward, and brethren of the

To have a governor.

said fraternity, &c. And that the queens will in the premises, may have a more excellent effect, she, fo. 143. assigneth, nameth, and createth, William Jennison, the elder, to be the first and modern governor, &c. fo. 144. Moreover she hath assigned, named, constituted, and appointed, Francis Anderson, and John Barker, to be the first and modern stewards of that fraternity, &c. fo. 145. 146. 147. 148. 149.

Power to make laws in their guild, as be pure, wholesome, good, and profitable, for the good government of the said company. * See 19 Hen. 7. 7.

(R) The queen further grants, to the said governor, stewards, and brethren of the said fraternity of hoast-men, &c. and to their successors, fo. 149. that the said governor, stewards, and brethren, &c. and their successors, &c. shall have in every fit time, for ever hereafter, full power of meeting, in their guild-hall, or in any other place convenient, within the said town, and there to constitute, make, fo. 150. such laws,* institutes, &c. which to the said governor, stewards, and brethren, &c. good, wholesome, profitable, &c. according as they shall think good, for the good rule and government of the governor, stewards, and brethren of the said fraternity, and for declaration,

by

by what means and order, they, fo. 151. and their factors, servants, and apprentices, in their office and bufineſſes, concerning the ſaid fraternity, they ſhall have, carry and uſe, &c. and that the governor, ſtewards, and brethren of that fraternity, &c. as often as they grant, make, ordain, or eſtabliſh ſuch laws, inſtitutes, inform, fo. 152. and they may impoſe ſuch pains, penalties,* puniſhments, and impriſonments* of body, or by fines, &c. upon all delinquents againſt ſuch laws, (s) inſtitutes, &c. as to them ſhall be thought neceſſary and requiſite, and as to them ſhall be thought beſt, for the obſervation of the ſaid laws, ordinances, &c. fo. 153. and the ſaid fines and amerciaments, at their diſcretions, they may levy, have. and retain, to them and their ſucceſſors, to the uſe of the governor, ſtewards, and brethren, aforeſaid, without calumny, &c. all which, and ſingular laws, ordinances, &c. the ſaid late queen willeth, to be obſerved; ſo that the ſaid laws, ordinances, fo. 154, &c. be not repugnant, to the laws, or ſtatutes, of the kingdom of England.

* See ſtat. 25. Ed. 1. 5. To impoſe penalties by fine or impriſonment upon the offender.
* See 28. Ed. 3. 3. And to have all fines for the company's uſe. See chap. 43. D. Such laws to be obſerved, if they be not repugnant to the known laws of England. See ſtat. 19. Hen. 77.

And further, the queen granteth, to the ſaid governor, ſtewards, and brethren, &c. and to their ſucceſſors, that for ever hereafter, they and their ſucceſſors, &c. fo. 155. may have, and ſhall have, full power, from time to time, at their pleaſure, to chuſe, name, and ordain, other inhabitants, and burgeſſes of the ſaid town, &c. to be, and ſhall be brethren of the ſaid fraternity, &c. who, ſo elected, nominated, and ſworn, ſhall be named, and be brethren of that fraternity.

Moreover, fo. 156. the ſaid queen grants licence, power, and authority, to the ſaid governor, ſtewards, and brethren, &c. and to their ſucceſſors, that they, for the time being, and their ſucceſſors, and every of them, for ever hereafter, may and ſhall, quietly and peaceably, have, hold, uſe, and enjoy, all ſuch liberties, privileges, &c. fo. 157. concerning the loading, and unloading, ſhipping,

*They to have all the loading or reloading of coals, &c. in that port, in any part of the port, notwithstanding the statute of the 21. Hen. 8. chap. 18. See stat. 21. Ja. 3. a monopoly.

It is conceived this charter could not repeal that statute.

or unshipping, of stone-coals, pit-coals*, grind-stones, rub-stones, and whet-stones, (T) And that they may for ever hereafter, load and unload, ship and unship, in or out of any ships or vessels, pit-coals, and stones aforesaid, within the said river and port of Tyne, in any place or places, as to them shall be expedient, fo. 158. between the said town of Newcastle, &c. and the aforesaid place, in the aforesaid river, called the Sparhawke, so nigh to the said town of Newcastle, &c. as conveniently may be done, according to the true intention of these letters pattents, as the men and brethren of the said fraternity, at any time, have used and accustomed, notwithstanding the statute of king Henry 8. the 3. of November, in the 21. year of his reign, and from thence adjourned to Westminster, holden, published, 1559. Intituled, An act concerning Newcastle, and the port, and, &c. to the same belonging, or any other act, &c. notwithstanding: And the said queen also willeth, &c. for that express mention, &c. witness the queen, at Westminster, the 22. of March, in the 13. year of her reign, fo. 160.

What a world of profits is given from the crown, which ought to maintain it, and would have so filled the coffers, as that there had been little need of sesments, &c.

Having read some works, of those late famous expositors of the law, I drew two or three heads out as observations, for the knowledge of those, who know them not, written by way of explanation of our known laws, as being a law, used time out of mind, or by prescription.

The law of nature is, that which God infused into the heart of man, for his preservation and direction, and that the law of England is grounded upon six principal points; the law of reason, the law of God, divers customs of this land, of divers principles and maxims, divers particular customs, and of divers statutes, made in parliament.

The

The fundamentall lawes of England are fo excellent, that they are the birth-right, and the moft antient and beft inheritance, that the free people of England have, for by them, they enjoy not onely their inheritance and goods, in peace and quietnefs, but their lives and dear country, in peace and fafety. Cooks preface to the fixth replication, and on Littleton, l. 2. c. 12. fect. 213.

Sometime it is called right, fometime common right, and fometimes *communis juftitia;* and it is the fame law which William the Conqueror found in England, the laws which he fware to obferve, were, *Bonæ, &c. approbatæ antiquæ regni legis.*

Charter-law being fo repugnant to the above written, and fo deftructive to the weal of the people, that never any writer ever writ of them, nor ever any parliament enacted their publication, knowing they were no other then prerogative, and dyes with the donor; and it is an infallible rule, where no law is publifhed, there cannot be any tranfgreffion, or obedience required.

The corporation of Newcaftle hath but two fupporters, to ftand and fall by, firft, prefcription, fecondly, cuftom.

As to prefcription, a quo warranto will avoid that upon a legall tryal, it being underftood, that charters are void, by reafon of the change of government, if not, yet by breach of charter, exceeding their power, being nothing elfe then a fallacy.

And as to plead cuftom, they have no right, nor never in poffeffion of what they claim; cuftomary right is good law, but cuftom without right, is but an old error, and ought to be removed; drunkennefs and fwearing is cuftomary: Is it fit it fhould ftand becaufe of its cuftom?

Kings were before corporations, and could have better juftified themfelves, for a continuance, then corporations, by reafon they might plead hereditary, or electary, conquerors, or cuftomary, yet being
found

found a grievance, was taken and removed for their arbitrary actings: Why then muft their power ftand, that is no law?

If it were juftice to execute thofe two judges, Empfon and Dudly, for onely putting a ftatute law in execution, not repealed, which is above charters, being grievous to the people; it were nothing more to execute juftice upon fuch, who act the fame without any law.

King John who was a murderer, yet commanded a murderer to be taken from the altar, and fent to the flaughter. Here was juftice!

Why do not our juft judges fend fuch like, from the charter to the flaughter? If Strafford loft his life for acting oppreffively, by an arbitrary power, why not others for the fame?

C H A P. XII.

KING JAMES,

His charters and orders.

MARS, FUER, ALECTO, VIRGO, VULPES, LEO, NULLUS.

(A) **K**ING JAMES, in the fecond year of his reign, being humbly fupplicated by the mayor, and burgeffes of Newcaftle, that he would be gracioufly pleafed, to confirm all their antient grants and charters, and to give them further powers, efpecially of the river Tyne, the king confirms their charters, but grants nothing new, onely alters the election of their officers, and prefcribes them new oathes, to be adminiftered to the faid officers, in their elections, which charter is in the chappel of rolls.

(B) Alfo

JAMES I.

(B) Alſo the king and his council, grants them the conſervancy of the river of Tyne, by giving nine articles, upon the 29. of January, 1613, and joyned in the ſaid order, the biſhop of Durham, and other juſtices of peace, of the county of Durham and Northumberland, with the ſix aldermen of the ſaid town of Newcaſtle; but three years after, being weary of partners, the mayor, aldermen, and a jury of the burgeſſes, exhibited a great complaint to the king and council, at White-hall, of the great decay of that river, occaſioned by the ſaid commiſſioners, through their neglect, and breach of truſt, which complaint, begat this following reference from the council table, and further power to add to the former. See chap. 34. (c.) 35. (A.B) 28. (A.P)

(c) Whereas, upon complaint of the decay of the river of Tyne, and of the daily abuſes, done and committed, to the prejudice of the ſame, certain articles were granted, on the 29. of January, 1613, and commanded to be put in execution, for the remedy of ſuch abuſes; and for as much as a jury of Newcaſtle-men, have, by their petition to this board, grievouſly complained thoſe articles were wholly neglected, by the mayor and ſix aldermen of the ſame town, and the biſhop of Durham, and juſtices of peace, all which were joynt commiſſioners, for the preſervation of that river, the river decaying ſo faſt, that in ſhort time, it would be dord and wrecked up, with ſand, &c. if not order ſoon taken therein. The council ordered ſir Ralph Winwood, ſir Julius Cæſar, and ſir Daniel Dunn, one of the judges of the admiralty, with the aſſiſtance of the trinity-maſters of London, to draw up thirteen articles more, to be joyned with the former nine. And by ſpecial order of his majeſties council, at White-hall, was given and commanded, that all the ſaid two and twenty articles, be put in execution, for the conſervation and preſervation of the river of Tyne, by the commiſſioners, hereafter

See chapters 19. 24. 25. 26. 28. 34. (A.B) 37. (A.B)

after named, or elſe to forfeit all the towns liberties, into the kings hands. See chap. 13.

(D) And though the commiſſioners, formerly appointed, for the execution of the former articles, are perſons of place and quality, and otherwiſe well deſerving of the publick, yet for as much as contrary to the truſt repoſed in them, they have altogether neglected their duty therein, whereof further notice may be taken, as occaſion ſhall require, it is thought expedient that theſe perſons following, be named and authorized commiſſioners, for the due performance and execution, as well of the ſaid former articles, bearing, date the 29. of January, 1613, as of thoſe now deviſed and publiſhed, with the joynt conſent, and good liking of the aldermen, of the town of Newcaſtle, and others attending their lordſhips, in that behalf, for the ſafety and conſervency of that river.

(E) *The names of the commiſſioners at Newcaſtle, for the river of Tyne.*

THE MAYOR,	JOHN HOLBOURN,
WILLIAM WARMOUTH,	HEN. JOHNSON,
TIMOTHY DRAPER,	EDW. FRENCH,
CUDB. BEWICK,	THO. EWBANK,
THO. WYNN,	GEORGE WALLIS,
LEO. CAR,	RALPH COX,
ROBERT LEGER,	JOHN EADEN,
JOHN STUBS,	JOHN BUTLER.
ROBERT CHAMBERLAIN,	

(F) 29. January, 1613.

See ſtat. 23. Hen. 8. 5.

1. THAT the owners of every ſalt-work, on either ſide of the river of Tyne, built and to be built, do, within ſix months build up their wharfs and keyes, ſufficiently above a full ſea-mark, in height of the water, to be appointed by the mayor, and ſix aldermen, to the end, neither coals nor rubbiſh do fall off into the river.

2. That

2. That all wharfs and keys, in all parts of the river of Tyne, be damm'd and back'd with earth, and not with ballaſt.

3. That no ballaſt be caſt at Shields, by any veſſel, which loadeth, either with coals or ſalt, or other commodities, nor any ballaſt wharfes to be built there, or uſed for that purpoſe. See chap. 19. (H), 24. (E), 18. (A).

4. That all ſalt-pan owners, ſhall carry away their pan rubbiſh, from off their keyes, or wharfs, every forty dayes, that none fall into the river.

5. That no ballaſt be caſt, but upon ſufficient ballaſt wharfs, built, and to be built, above a high water mark, and to be allowed by the mayor, and ſix aldermen, in any part of the river. See chap. 49. (G).

6. That the ſurveyors, unladers, and caſters of ballaſt, according to their offices and duties, ſhall, every week, cauſe all the ballaſt which falls off the ballaſt ſhores, into the river, to be taken up again, and caſt upon the ballaſt wharfs; and to take care, that the ſhips have a good fayl, to lie between the ſhip and ſhore, that none of the ballaſt fall between, into the river. See chap. 49. (G), 14. (B), 34. 35.

7. That no coals nor ſtones be digged, within ſixty yards, on a ſtreight line, from a full ſea-mark, in any part of the river, to the end none fall in.

8. That ſome ſtrict and ſevere puniſhment, be inflicted, by the mayor and ſix aldermen, upon any ſuch maſter of ſhip, or keels, as ſhall preſume to caſt any ballaſt, upon any inſufficient ſhores, or into the river. See chap. 49. (E), 39. 14. (C).

9. That there ſhall be no wyers, dams, or other ſtoppage, or caſting of ballaſt, in or neer the ſaid river, or creeks, running into the ſaid river of Tyne, or within eight miles of the town of Newcaſtle, but ſuch as ſhall be allowed, by the mayor and ſix aldermen, of the ſaid town, ſuch ſhores being ſufficiently wharfed. See chap. 34.

G *Thirteen*

Thirteen articles more granted, Feb. 14. 1616.

10. That no lighters, boats, or keels, with ballaſt, be ſuffered to go up and down, the river of Tyne, in any night tide, to prevent the keelmens caſting ballaſt into the river, they often uſing ſo to do, being more eaſie, and leſs labour to caſt it into the river, than upon the top of the ballaſt ſhores, which ſpoyls the river, the commiſſioners are to take care herein, to ſee the putting hereof, in execution, and to puniſh offenders. See chap. 49. (E).

11. That ſtrangers ſhall be appointed every week, to cleanſe the ſtreets in Newcaſtle, of their aſhes and other rubbiſh, to prevent the rain from waſhing the ſame into the river, thorough Loadbourn.

12. That all the gates, on the town key, be locked up every night, except one, or two, to ſtand open, for the maſters and ſea-men, to go too and fro, to their ſhips, which will prevent ſervants caſting aſhes, and other rubbiſh, into the river; and that thoſe two gates be conſtantly watched, all night long. See chap. 49. (F.), chap. 14. (B).

13. That all ſervants dwelling, with any the inhabitants, reſiding or inhabiting, in the town of Gates-head, and ſand-gate, and the cloſe, in Newcaſtle, be ſworn every year, not to caſt any rubbiſh, into the river. See chap. 49. (E).

14. Whereas there hath been an ancient cuſtome in Newcaſtle, that every maſter of any ſhip, who is known to caſt any ballaſt at ſea, between Souter and Hartly, or within fourteen fathom water of the haven, to the hurt of the ſaid river, was brought into the town chamber; and there in the preſence of the people, had a knife put into his hand, was conſtrained to cut a purſe, with monies in it, as who ſhould ſay he had offended in as high a degree, as if he cut a purſe from the perſon of a man, whereby he might be ſo aſhamed, that he ſhould never offend again therein; and others by his example, were

terrified

terrified from trespassing, in the like kind, that now in the time of so general wrongs, done to the river, and the great number of ships, which comes into that haven, this ancient custome be revived, and put in execution. See stat. 8. Eliz. 4. See chap. 39. (A).

15. That whereas much ballast falls off into the river of Tyne, between the ships and the ballast shores, in casting of it out of the ship, to the great hurt of the same, the commissioners are to set, every winter season, the poor keelmen, and shewel-men, on work, to cast into keels, such ballast and sand, fallen into the river, and then to cast it on the shores, or wharf again.

16. That some trusty truly substantial men, burgesses of Newcastle, be appointed to view the river, every week, and to make oath, for the abuses and wrongs, done unto the same, two to be masters of the trinity-house, of that town; they to have no coals, nor mines, nor ballast-shores, and to be appointed by the commissioners. See chap. 39. (35.)

17. That every owner of ground, adjoyning on that river, be ordered to fence the same grounds, to prevent the banks from falling, and washing into the river, with the great floods, flashes, and rains, to the great annoyance thereof. See chap. 49. (E).

18. That the commissioners, namely, the mayor, and others named before, do give unto the masters, skippers of keels, a commission, to be a company, for the ordering such their brotherhood, and for them to punish such, as cast ballast into the river, or doth other wrong, out of their keels, they having been a company formerly, consisting of one hundred and sixty, which was for the good of the river; that the two great pools of water, lying on the back of a ballast-shore, be forthwith filled up, to prevent undermining of the shore, to the hazard of the river, if the wall, and ballast fall down.

19. That

19. That all the ballaſt ſhores, in the river of Tyne, be conſtantly kept in good repair, otherwiſe, a hundred thouſand tons of ballaſt, will fall into the river, to the deſtruction thereof. See chap. 34.

20. That no ſhip or veſſel be ſuffered to load at Shields, or any road-ſtead in the river, but as neer the town of Newcaſtle, as can be, for when they load in remote places, the wrongs cannot be ſo ſoon ſeen. See chap. 19. (H), 24. (E).

21. That the commiſſioners do take good bonds, from the owners of ſuch ſhores, as ſhall be built, to lay coals on for ſhips, and ſhall take view of ſuch places, as ſhall not do hurt to the ſaid river,* either by caſting ballaſt on them, indirectly, or to ſuffer them to go to decay, after there is no uſe made of them, and to keep the ballaſt, from waſhing into the river. See chap. 13. 34. 35.

*Theſe articles are all void notwithſtanding it is all the power they can claim.

Theſe were preſent in council, that granted theſe articles.

LORD ARCHBISHOP OF CANTERBURY,	LORD ZOUCH,
	LORD CAREW,
LORD CHANCELLOR,	MR. COMPTROLER,
LORD TREASURER,	MR. VICE-CHAMBERLAIN
LORD STEWARD,	MR. SEC. WINDWOOD,
LORD ARRUNDEL,	MR. SECRETARY LAKE,
LORD CHAMBERLAIN,	MR. CHANCELLOR
LORD ADMIRAL,	EXCHEQUER,
EARLE BUCKINGHAM,	MR. OF THE ROLLS,
LORD BISHOP OF ELY,	MR. ATTORNEY GENERAL.

All theſe articles are broke, except the fifth, for cutting purſes, and the ninth article, in ſtopping up the two pools, &c. Read the following order, &c.

The council table ordered, that Leonard Car, and Cuthbert Beuwick, two of the commiſſioners which attend this buſineſſe, be allowed their charges, for their pains and attendance, and likewiſe this board might be the better aſſured, with what care and diligence theſe directions are purſued, that the commiſſioners,

do

do every quarter certifie, of the proceedings herein, that further order might be taken, upon any defect that might happen, and as shall be found expedient.

CHAP. XIII.

An order to feize all Newcaftles liberties, &c.

UPON an order, now taken, concerning the river of Tyne, and divers articles, conceived fit by the board, for the preventing of such diforders, and abufes, as are done, and committed, to the detriment of the faid river, it is thought fit, and fo ordered, for the better obfervancy of the faid articles, and the more carefull endeavours of the mayor, and aldermen, of the town of Newcaftle, for the reformation, and amendment, of such things, as are hurtfull and prejudicial to fo famous a river, which have been flighted and neglected, beyond that, which any way may be reafonably thought of, in a matter of fo great importance.

That upon the firft juft complaint, renewed to this board, in that kind, his majefties attorney general be hereby authorifed, without further queftion, or warrant, to direct fome courfe, for the feizing of all the liberties of that town, into the kings hand; of which their lordfhips pleafure and refolution, is, that fuch aldermen, and others of that town, as are now here attending that bufinelfe, were by the board required, hereby to take notice. Given at our court, at Whitehall, this 16. of February, 1616. See chap. 19. (A), 24. (A), 25. (A), 26. (A), 28. (A), 34. (A), 35. (A.B).

There

There were thefe prefent in council.

LORD ARCHBISHOP OF CANTERBURY,	MR. COMPTROLER,
LORD CHAMBERLAIN,	MR. VIC. CHAMBERLAIN,
LORD ARRUNDEL,	MR. SEC. WINDWOOD,
LORD VIC. WALLINGFORD,	MR. SEC. LAKE,
LORD STEWARD,	MR. CHANCELLOR EXCHEQUER,
LORD BISHOP OF ELY,	MASTER OF THE ROLLS,
LORD ZOUCH,	MR. ATTORNEY GENERAL.

It is conceived a writ of feizure, lyes in this cafe, by reafon of the many grievous complaints, exhibited for their exorbitant abufes, committed againft the weal of the nation, in that river, in the fpoyl thereof, as appears, and in not putting all thofe articles in execution, for prefervation thereof, &c.

In Michaelmas, 1643, in the prefence of Mr. Juftice Snape, fteward of the liberties of St. Katherines, London, the lord chief juftice, St. John, did direct to feize St. Katherines liberties, for not yeelding obedience, to a writ of the common bench, executed in St. Katherines, and the attorney that gave the advice was committed. (A good precedent.)

CHAP. XIV.

A return, by the commiffioners of Newcaftle, in the due execution of their power, &c.

(A) THE commiffioners, for confervency of the river of Tyne, at Newcaftle, returns their quarterly account, of their diligent care, in the due execution, of the two and twenty articles, afore-mentioned, unto the council table, by Mr. Leon. Car,

and

and Mr. Buewick, with order to petition the council, for an explanation, upon fome of the faid two and twenty articles, and for further power, for the prefervation of the faid river, efpecially upon the one and twentieth article, to whom the bonds fhould be made. It was ordered to the mayor, for the time being, &c.

(B) Alfo prayed refolution, who fhould repair and maintain the ballaft fhoars, and coal-wharf, as is expreft in the nineteenth article. Ordered, that as well the owner as the tenant, be bound to fuch reparation, during the time ufe was made thereof, and onely the owners afterwards.

They alfo humbly craved their refolutions of the fixth article, and twelfth article, who fhould be at the charge of cleanfing the river, of the ballaft, and pay the watchmen, &c. It is ordered, that the town-chamber, defray both the one, and the other, by reafon, they receive the profits of the river, &c. See chap. 12. (6), chap. 34. 39. 49.

(c) They alfo prayed the refolution of the eighth article, for the punifhing of mafters of fhips. It was ordered, that the commiffioners fhould take bond, with fufficient fureties, to appear before the council, to anfwer their contempt, and to fuch as refufe to give bond, then the commiffioners, to commit them to prifon, till they give fureties, to anfwer at London, &c. See chap. 41. (c).

Ordered, that the commiffioners fhall have power, for ordering the wharf, and new fhoars, in every place, in that river, after they are once erected, as well for the ftrengthning as backing of them, with ballaft, as with other earth. See chap. 18. (v).

(E) That the commiffioners, there at leaft, fhall fubfcribe every ticket, and the mayor, for the carrying up of every keel of ballaft, from the fhips at Shields, to Newcaftle ballaft fhoars, for the more faithfull execution of that fervice. See chap. 49. (G).

(F) Ordered, that the commiffioners fhall have power, to order and determine, of fuch rewards, as

fhall

shall be given, to every wherry-man, or fisherman, or other, that shall truly present any offence, or offenders, against any of the articles prescribed, to be taken out of such fines, mulcts and amerciaments, as shall be imposed upon any the delinquents, against the said articles. See chap. 39. (A).

(G) Ordered, that the commissioners shall have power, to cause the ballast, already become noysome, or in any part of the river, or like to do hurt, from the land, to be removed to a new wharf, or fit place. See chap. 34. (A), 35. (A.B.).

CHAP. XV.

KING JAMES, on the 14. of April, in the seventeenth year of his reign, grants unto Alexander Stevenson, Esq. and his assigns, for fifty years, the whole castle of Newcastle, with all appurtenances thereunto, any way belonging, at the rent of forty shillings, per annum. except the prison, wherein is kept the sons of Belial, it being the county prison, for Northumberland; the said Mr. Stevenson dyed, and left Mr. Auditor Darel, his executor, and left him that lease, it being all he was like to have, towards the payment of the said Mr. Stevensons debts, which was due to the said executor, and others, amounting in the principle, to two thousand and five hundred pound, besides damages, which amounted to as much more, who is kept from his right, by the instigation of the mayor and burgesses, upon an inquisition taken, the 18. of August, in the 18. year of king James, at Newcastle. It was found to be in Stevenson, and now in his executors. The said Stevenson dyed in October, 1640, they claiming a right from one widow Langston,

Langſton, relict to one John Langſton, groom, porter, &c. but that title, the law will quickly decide, upon a legal trial; but the county of Northumberland hath the reverſion, who is kept, from having a free paſſage to the aſſizes, by the mayor and burgeſſes, who ſhuts up the gates, which is the right paſſage, and at ſuch gates, which be open, the people of Northumberland, coming to do their ſervice, at the aſſizes, holden for that county, in that caſtle, are arreſted, and caſt into priſon, by Newcaſtle, where none can bail them, but burgeſſes of Newcaſtle, and often thereby, ſuch people, have their cauſe overthrown, by ſuch reſtrainment.

In eaſter term, in the 18. year of king James, ſir Henry Yelverton, kt. attorney general, exhibited an information, againſt the mayor and burgeſſes, concerning the premiſes above mentioned, where all plainly appears, amongſt other things of the town, not to belong to them, &c.

CHAP. XVI.

(A) IN or about the eighteenth year of king James, an information was exhibited, in the Star Chamber, by the attorney general, againſt the mayor, and burgeſſes of Newcaſtle, by the name of hoſtmen, for that they, having the preemption of coals, from the inheritors in Northumberland, and county of Durham, by their charter of free-hoaſt-men, 42. queen Elizabeth,* they having the ſale of all coals, who force ſhips to take bad coals, or will not load them, with unmarketable coals, being brought for London, prove much to the damage of the people.

Which grief begot great ſuits, between the merchants, and maſters of ſhips, to their diſquieting and high charge, upon which, this information was
brought

brought againſt the ſaid hoaſt-men, for ſelling of bad and unmerchantable coals, and much ſlate amongſt them; for which they were all fined, ſome 100l. a peece, ſome more, others leſs; being found guilty, and ordered to do ſo no more; but it is proved, they continue the ſame, to this day. See chap. 43. (A.).

CHAP. XVII.

(A.) **KING JAMES**, upon the 28th. of January, in the 16. year of his reign, grants the admiralty, of all England, &c. to the duke of Buckingham, it being ſurrendred by the lord high admiral, ſo that the title of Newcaſtle, by vertue of the charter. of the 31. year of queen Elizabeths reign, is conceived of little force. See chap. 10. (B).

CHAP. XVIII.

KING CHARLES

HIS ORDERS.

(A.) **SIR ROBERT HEATH**, lord chief juſtice of the common pleas, was building a ballaſt wharf, or ſhoar, on his own land, at Shields, adjoyning upon the river of Tyne, ſeven miles from Newcaſtle; but the commiſſioners of Newcaſtle, the mayor and aldermen, with others, obſtructed the building thereof, pretending it would ſpoil the river; but the lord chief juſtice, well knowing it to the contrary, by the advice of moſt of the antient trinity

CHARLES I.

trinity mafters, of London, and other experienced traders thither, went on with the building thereof, upon which, in the year 1632, the faid mayor, and other commiffioners, exhibited a complaint, to the king and council, againft the fame, at Whitehall, complaining, that, if any ballaft fhoars, or wharfs, were built, at Shields, it would much fpoil the river, and hinder trade and navigation; at which there was a legal tryal. It appeared to the contrary. The king and council, upon the 13th. day of July, 1632, ordered, that Sir Robert Heaths ballaft fhoar, fhould be built.

(D) In February next, the commiffioners of Newcaftle, complained again, upon the fame bufinefs, by pleading fome new matter, in their petition, and the reference they obtained, on their petition, was ordered, by the king and council, this 13th. of February, 1632, that fir Robert Heaths ballaft fhoar fhould be built. The commiffioners aforefaid, put in the third petition, not doubting, but that by fuch new matter, they fhould prevent the building of the faid fhoar. Ordered, by the king and council, the 27. Feb. 1632, that fir Robert Heaths ballaft fhoar, wharf, or key, a building, fhall be built, go forward, and be quite finifhed. See chap. 13. (A), 19. (A), 20. (C), 34. (A.B.).

CHAP. XIX.

THE mayor and burgeffes exhibited another great complaint, to the king and council, wherein nine feveral abfurdities appeared, by capt. Crofier, and efpecially againft fir Rob. Heaths fhoar, &c.

A RESOLVE OF THE COUNCIL.

At the court, at Greenwich, the 1. of June, 1634.

KING CHARLES,

LORD ARCHBISHOP OF CANTERBURY,	LORD CHAMBERLAIN,
LORD KEEPER,	EARL OF DORSET,
LORD ARCHBISHOP OF YORK,	EARL OF BRIDGEWATER,
	LORD VI. WIMBLETON,
LORD TREASURER,	LORD NEWBROUGH,
LORD PRIVY-SEAL,	MR. TREASURER.
LORD DUKE OF LENOX,	MR. COMPTROLLER,
LORD MARQUIS HAMBLETON,	MR. VICE CHAMBERLAIN,
	MR. SEC. WINDWOOD,
	MR. SEC. COOK.

Upon confideration, this day had, at the board, his majefty being prefent in council, of a complaint made, by the mayor, and burgeffes of Newcaftle, againft the ballaft-fhoars, lately built, by the faid fir Robert Heath, at Shields, upon the river of Tyne, pretending the fame to be a great prejudice, of the fhipping and navigation, and to the annoyance, and damage of the faid river, the care and confideration thereof, was, by his majefty, efpecially intrufted unto them, (E) and upon hearing the allegation, on both fides, with their learned council, in the law, it was thought fit, and ordered, that the faid fhoar fhould be finifhed, and backed with ballaft, to make it fit for the falt works, which for his majefties fervice, are begun, and intended to be performed. (G).

In the firft place, that the feamen fhould have liberty, freely to caft their ballaft there, (H) without interruption, if they find convenient, none being compelled to it, or hindred from it. That neither thofe of the town of Newcaftle, nor free hoaft-men (I) (which fell all coals) do hinder the fame, indirectly, by denying, or unneceffary denying, to carry down coals, in keels, or lighters, to the fhips, which fhall caft their ballaft, at that fhoar, to the end,

end, this shoar, which may be for the safety, and incouragement, of navigation and shipping, may be so used, as the same, may neither be prejudicial to the town, in diverting or withdrawing of trade, nor to his majesty, in his customs or duty, nor hurtful to the said river.

His majesty will refer the ordering hereof, to himself, as well in the particulars aforesaid, as in all other things, thereunto appertaining, in such sort, as both the town and seamen, shall find his majesties regall care over them. *Sic subscripsit ex. majest.* See 12, chap. 3. 18. (D.F), 23. (A), 42. (E).

It is conceived, orders are no laws, and the latter order, which contradicts the former, voids it; so by this of king Charles, voids king James's for the power of the river, in chap. 12. (1).

CHAP. XX.

Jarrow Slike; &c.

(A) ON the 4th. of December, 1634, certain lands, and wastes were discovered, to the late kings commissioners, at the commission-house, in fleet-street, as belonging to the crown, concealed, especially, a parcel of land, or waste, in the river of Tyne, called Jarrow-slike, at South-Shields, in the county of Durham, which the water, at a full sea, covers every tide, and is by estimation, 300 acres, a fit and convenient place, for ships to cast ballast at; for many years to come, without any prejudice to the river, and great furtherance of trade. See chap. 56. chap. 34. (A.B.).

The mayor and burgesses of Newcastle, hearing thereof, put in their claim, to the said commissioners, and alledged, that all that ground belonged to them, with all other grounds, to a low water mark, from the full sea-mark, on both sides the river, from a place called Sparhawke, in the sea, to Headwyn-streams, which is seven miles above Newcastle, being fourteen miles in length, granted to them, and their heirs, for ever, from king John by charter, and confirmed by his successors; and therefore beseeched time, to make it so appear. (There being no such thing granted, could never make it appear.) A long time was given them, but nothing appeared, as truth of any such grant, and two years after, upon the first day of July, 1637, they instead of wearying out the commissioners, and gentlemen, that discovered the same, was called to make good their claim. Then they became petitioners to the kings commissioners, that they would be pleased, to sell that parcel of waste ground, called Jarrow-flike, to them, and to admit them to purchase the same, for which they would give two hundred pounds, by reason, it lay more convenient for them, then any else but they would give no more money for it. See chap. 18. (A.B). See chap. 2.

Upon which, one Mr. Thomas Talbot, and Mr. Richard Allen, of London, gave four hundred pound, and got it. The king upon the 27. of November, 1637, by his letters pattents, under the great seal of England: confirmed the same Jarrow-flike, and waste ground, upon the said Talbot and Allen, and their heirs, for ever; they paying in to the exchequer five pound per annum, as a fee-farm rent, which said ground, is in contest, between the said Gentlemen, and sir Henry Vane.

If this ground, to a full sea-mark, were really the corporation of Newcastles, it would have so appeared in the charter, granted by king John, and also, they then, might have made good their claim, and not to have become petitioners, to purchase the thing, which was their own before; even as they do in this, so in other things.

Alſo, if all ground be theirs, from a full ſea-mark, why were they tenants to the late dean, and chapters, of Durham, of certain ballaſt ſhores, built to the low water-mark, on which all ballaſt is caſt.

And if all ground were Newcaſtles, from a full ſea-mark, why ſhould Mr. Bonner, &c. buy the lady Gibs ground, and build a ballaſt-ſhoar, to a low water-mark, and wrong the town of their right; and why ſhould not Gates-head, and both the Shields, which are built to a low water-mark, pay Newcaſtle rent, &c. See chap. 18. (B), 34. (A.B.).

C H A P. XXI.

(A) KING Charles, in Auguſt, in the 13. year of his reign, created a new corporation, of free hoſt-men, in Newcaſtle, (called in engliſh, coale-engroſſers) and grants a leaſe, to ſir Thomas Tempeſt, knight, with others, for the ſelling of all coals, exported out of the river of Tyne, and to receive eleven ſhillings and four pence, per chaldron, cuſtome, and twelve ſhillings, from all ſtrangers, which ſhall be tranſported over ſea, and to have two pence, per chaldron, towards their charge, and power to ſeize of all coals, ſold by the owners of ſuch coals, ſold; in which leaſe, it is ordered, that if maſters of ſhips have not their due meaſure, at one and twenty boulls, to the chaldron, then upon information given, the one half of ſuch coals, and keels, to be forfeited to ſuch maſter, and the meaſures to be looked after, by ſworn commiſſioners, and that this leaſe (monopoly) to continue, for one and twenty years, from January, then laſt paſt, and that nothing be done or acted, by pretence, or colour of this leaſe, to the prejudice of the king. See chap. 11. (P.), 8. (A.). See ſtat. 21. king James 3. See chap. 46. (B.).

It is conceived this leaſe is void, both by law, &c.

If

If any such prejudice the people, the king is also prejudiced here, the people cannot sell their own coals, &c. which is a prejudice. See his oath, chap. 59. (A.).

CHAP. XXII.

(A) KING Charles, in June following, in the fourteenth year of his reign, incorporates another company of coal buyers, namely Mr. Tho. Horth, and other masters of ships, to buy all coals, exported out of the ports of Sunderland, the river of Tyne, Newcastle, Blith, and Barwick, paying to the king, one shilling, per chaldron, custome, and to sell them again, to the city of London, not exceeding seventeen shillings the chaldron, in the summer, and nineteen shillings the chaldron, all the winter; provided they had a free market, and a just measure, at Newcastle, &c. which they were debarred of, by reason of the foregoing lease, granted to sir Thomas Tempest. See chap. 11. (P).

CHAP. XXIII.

(A) KING Charles, in July following, grants another pattent, to Mr. Sands, with others, for the farming of the customes, of one shilling, aforesaid, upon every chaldron, at the yearly rent of ten thousand pounds. By this, you may see, no small quantity issues out, &c. See chap. 11. (B).

But there are some other gentlemen, which hath this benefitial lease at present, namely sir John Trevor

vor, with others, who payes (as I hear) one thoufand four hundred pound, per annum, (having fome yeers yet to come in the pattent). I wifh the poor had it after them, at the rent of five thoufand pounds, per annum. And it is the judgement of wife men, that thofe gentlemen, are wanting of many hundreds of pounds, per annum, which might be made, as well as the former, &c.

CHAP. XXIV.

Die Jovis, Octob. 8. 1646.

By the committee of lords and commons, for the admiralty, and cinque ports, &c.

WHEREAS, the committee hath been petitioned, by Barbery Hilton, widow, on the behalf of herfelf, and divers mafters of fhips, trading to Newcaftle, whofe names are here fubfcribed, to the faid petition, that the petitioners may receive the benefit, of loading, and unloading, at the ballaft-wharf, erected at Shields, about feven miles from Newcaftle, as tending to the good, and prefervation of fhipping, &c. for that by reafon, the river is wrecked up, with fands, and funk fhips, that fhips of great burdens cannot paffe up, without hazard, and danger of lofing, which liberty, as by their petition is fet forth, they enjoyed for fixteen yeers paft, untill of late, the mayor and commonalty of Newcaftle, have enforced them to come up, to their own fhoars.

Now, for as much as this matter, as it is reprefented unto the committee, may tend much to the fecurity of fhips, the advancement of navigation, and encouragement of trade, (E).

I It

It is ordered therefore, that the petitioners shall be at liberty, to load and unload, at the Shields, as is defired, and directed, untill other order, in that behalf be given.

And if the magiftrates of Newcaftle, and fuch others, as is therein concerned, fhall hereafter defire, to offer reafons to the contrary, this committee will be ready to hear them, and to do therein, what fhall ftand with juftice. See chap. 19. (G.H.1).

WARWICK,	ESQ. BENCE,
ALEX. BENCE,	ED. PRIDEAUX,
SALISBURY,	GILES GREEN.
JO. ROLI.,	

It is conceived, this order voids king James orders, for prefervation of the river, in the two and twenty articles, and confirms king Charles, &c. See chap. 19.

CHAP. XXV.

At the council for trade, at White-hall, Sept. 26. 1651.

(A) IN purfuance of a reference of the council of ftate, of the 8. of Feb. 1650. to take into confideration, the petition of fome captains and mafters of fhips, with others trading to Newcaftle, with a paper of their grievances, annexed to the fame, fetting forth, &c. See 12. chap. the 19. and 24. chap.

(B) That

(B) That in cafe of any difafter to fhips, after extremity of weather, or otherwife, though in great diftreffe. See chap. 29. (c), 30. (A.D.S), 33. (A).

(c) Are debarred to take the affiftance, and help of any other neighbouring fhip-wrights, and carpenters of their own hired fervants, who they have entertained in their fhips, for their fhip-carpenters. See chap. 36. (A), 38. (c).

(D) But are conftrained, either to carry their fhips, to Newcaftle, or to remain there in peril, till one be fent for, or procured from Newcaftle, who will not come upon reafonable terms. See chap. 30. (B), 38. (A.B).

(E) Complaining alfo, that the town will not fuffer them, according to ancient liberties, and cuftomes, to heave, and caft out ballaft, at convenient and fufficient fhoars, where they may do it, without endangering their fhips. See chap. 29. (c), 30. (A), 32. (D), 35. (B), 41. (A), 43. (D), 44. (A).

(F) Nor to load, nor unload, where they may with fafety perform it, notwithftanding fome orders, heretofore, to that end obtained, from the late king, and from the parliament; but are moft injurioufly forced, to carry up their fhips, to Newcaftle, through moft dangerous parts of the river, by reafon of fands, fhelves, and divers* funk fhips, in the way, with other particulars, to the like purpofe.

(H) The council, having taken the faid papers, into confideration, and it appearing, that the faid town of Newcaftle, however they juftifie not the hindring of any mafter, to make ufe of his own hired fhip-carpenter, coming along with him, in the faid fhip, do, notwithftanding, juftifie the hindring of any other fhip-carpenter, to work or affift him, if not a free-man of their town, and do claim the fole imployment of their own free fhip-wrights, within the whole port, of the faid town. See chap. 12. (1), 29. (c,),

29. (C), 31. (A), 34, (C), 32. (C.B.), 35. (A.B.), 38. (A), 49. (A), 50. (C).

(I) As alfo do juſtiſie the fole erection, keeping, and heaving, of all the ballaſt-ſhoars, within the faid port, (K), and the hindring any perfon, to load or unload, at any place of the faid port, fave at the faid town, or as near it as conveniently may be.

(L) This council, having further received the depofitions, and examinations, of feveral mariners, and maſters of ſhips, belonging to the town of Newcaſtle, and others alfo, of the town of Ipfwich; and having alfo advifed, with fome maſters of ſhips, antient and experienced traders, fent and chofen, by the trinity-houfe, of London, with fome others, do, after full debate had, and hearing, at divers meetings, the reafons on both fides alledged, offer, fee chap. 33. (A), 38. (A.B), 56. (A).

(M) That the faid practice, of the faid town of Newcaſtle, in debarring maſters of ſhips, to make ufe, within the river of Tyne, of what ſhip-carpenters they pleafe, or find fitteſt for their own conveniency, and in conſtraining them to ufe onely the free ſhip-wrights, of the faid town of Newcaſtle, is very prejudicial to trade and navigation. See chap. 33. (A), 38. (A.B.C).

(N) That it hath appeared to this council, notwithſtanding any thing to the contrary, alledged, &c. that through the winds, rains, and other cafualties, waſhing down the ballaſt of thofe, that are called the town of Newcaſtles ſhoars, having been a great newfance, and prejudice, to the river, and in the higher parts thereof. See chap. 34. (C), 35. (A.B).

(O) And that the practice of the faid town of Newcaſtle, in conſtraining the faid maſters of ſhips, to come up the river, and to heave out their ballaſt, at the town ſhoars only, (P), and hindring them to load coals, and difcharge their ballaſt, where they may with fafety perform it, as well to the road-ſtead

it

itfelf, as to their fhipping, is a damage and inconveniency to trade and navigation. See ch. 34. (c), 44. (A), 41. (A), 44. (E), 32. (D), 43. (D), 29. (C), 31. (A).

(Q) To hinder any fhips, to buy or take in, at any place of the faid port, bread and beer, for their own fpending, and victualling, is alfo a very great hinderance, to trade and navigation. See chap. 48. (A), 49. (C.D.G), 50. (A), 51 (B), 44. (E), 29. (A).

(R) That notwithftanding, for the better regulating fuch further liberties, as fhall be granted, in the granting of the faid provifions, building of ballaftfhoars, defraying the charge, and for the prefervation of the river, for the future, be intrufted into faithful, able mens hands, to fee the fame put in execution, as to the wifdom of the parliament, fhall be thought fit, &c.

JOHN JOHNSON, clerk. pro tempore.

CHAP. XXVI.

A judgement at the common law, obtained againft Newcaftle, &c.

(A) THOMAS CLIFF, a fhip-carpenter, who hath been very inftrumental, in faving many fhips from finking, and at eafie rates, for his working upon a fhip, in the fame river of Tyne, in the year 1646, had got a fhip, off the rocks, with the help of his fervants, and other work-men, for which, the mayor and burgeffes of Newcaftle, fent down fergeants, with other burgeffes, to the town of North-Shields, which is in the county of Northumberland, to bring the faid Cliff, and fervants, to their prifon; in which fervice, the faid fergeants killed his wife, brake his

his daughters arm, and led his servants to prison,* as you may read, chap. 36. and then sued the said Cliff, by an english bill, in the exchequer, and held him in suit, five years and upwards, the suit being commenced, in the name of the mayor and burgesses of Newcastle, complainants, against Tho. Cliff, defendant. The merchants and burgesses, of that corporation, came in as witnesses, in their own cause, as you may find upon record, in the exchequer, where they were examined, in the year 1649, Jan. 27. by vertue of a commission, &c. also they were cross examined, &c. which said suit, was transferred to the common law, and to be tryed at York assizes, in hillary, 1651. The verdict went for the defendant, Cliff; which said judgement expresses, that the mayor and burgesses ought to be severely fined, &c. for their unjust claim, in that port of the river of Tyne, and shall pay 30l. costs, &c. which said bill is in the office of pleas, in Lincolns-Inn, &c. See chap. 19. (c), 24. (A), 25. (A), 54. 28.

CHAP. XXVII.

To the supream authority, the parliament of the commonwealth of England.

The humble petition of Ralph Gardner, of Northumberland, gent. in behalf of himself and many others, whose desires are thereunto annexed, &c.

Sheweth,

(A) THAT many great complaints, of grievances and oppressions, presented to the council of state, in the year 1650, in writings, by many captains, and masters of ships, with others, against the magistrates of Newcastle upon Tyne, in relation to trade and navigation.

The council of ſtate, by order, transferred the ſame to be examined, by the council for trade, and after a long debate, at ſeveral times, divers witneſſes were ſworn, and counſel had on both ſides.

The council for trade, drew up a report thereupon, to preſent to the parliament, conducing much to the good of trade, and navigation, which ſaid report hath lyen dormant, ever ſince, to the great detriment of the commonwealth, in the exceſſive prizes of coales, and otherwiſe.

Your petitioner humbly prays, that thoſe reports and papers, may be called for, and reviewed, and theſe annexed deſires inſerted, to do therein, as to your wiſedoms and juſtice, ſhall ſeem meet,

And as in duty bound, ſhall pray, &c.
RALPH GARDNER.

Henry Ogle,
29. Sept. 1653.

Gardners deſires to the parliament.

(B) THAT North-Shields be made a market town, it being ſeven miles from Newcaſtle, and twelve miles from any market, in the ſame county, which would relieve the garriſon of Tinmouth caſtle, the inhabitants, which be thouſands, the great confluence of people reſorting thither, the great fleets of ſhips daily riding there; would further them to make many more voyages in the year, ſave boats and mens lives, which are often in danger of being caſt away, in ſtormy weather*; alſo, by which means, the people would be relieved with proviſions, during the time the river is frozen, and half in half cheaper, than from the ſecond hand; beſides the loſs of a daies labour, and great charge to the poor, in going by water, in boat-hire; and ſave the life of many a man and beaſt, from falling into coal-pits, which lies open, after the coals wrought out; being covered
with

with fnow, &c. See chap. 29. (A), 48. (A), 49. (B), 50. (A), 51. (A).

(c) That the mayor and burgeffes, may no more imprifon poor artificers, onely for working upon their trades, in or about the river. See chap. 36. (A), 38. (A.C).

(D) That they may not caft men into prifon, for faving of fhips from finking, nor keep men in prifon, till they give them bond, never to work upon their trade again. See chap. 33. (A) 36. (A), 38. (A).

(E) That they may not force all goods, brought in by fea for the falt and coal-works ufe, at and near the Shields, to be carryed up to Newcaftle, where there is no ufe, for the fame. See chap. 50.

(F) That the coal owners of Northumberland, and county of Durham, may have free liberty, to fell their own coals to fhips, and not to be inflaved, by the free hoaft-men, of the town of Newcaftle.

(G) That any perfon may have liberty, to build fhips and veflels, in the river of Tyne, without the moleftation of the magiftrates, of the town of Newcaftle, for the increafe of trade and navigation.

(H) That no mafters of fhips may be imprifoned, for refufing to fwear againft themfelves, according to the practice of the Star-chamber, it being a great difcouragement to trade, and difquieting of the fpirits, of many confcientious perfons, &c. See chap. 39. (A), 49.

(I) That all unreafonable, and arbitrary fines, may be mitigated, as fhall be agreeable to juftice, and equity. See chap. 41. 42. (A).

(K) That no more fhips may be compelled, up the dangerous river, feven miles, whereas, they need to go but one mile; never any coals, being to be had at Newcaftle, which would fave many fhips from finking, and caufe them to make upwards of three voyages in the year more than they do, which would caufe, two or three hundred thoufand chaldron of coals more to be fold, and the excefive prices to

fall,

fall under twenty shillings the chalder, all the year. See chap. 29. (c), 32. (c), 31. (a).

(L) That the truſt of the river of Tyne, be put into faithfull commiſſioners hands, the mayor, and aldermen, and commiſſioners of Newcaſtle, having betrayed the truſt, repoſed in them, for conſervancy thereof; that whereas within this twenty years, above twenty ſhips, of the burden two hundred tuns, rid afloat, in moſt road-ſteads, in the ſaid river, now, not above four, of the ſame burden, at low water. See chap. 12. (1), 34. (c.), 35. (A.B.).

(M) That their charters, granted to their corporation, may be called in, and viewed, and other grants and orders, granted by king James; and what is found offenſive to the commonwealth, may be repealed; as it now ſtands, proves deſtructive to the peoples right. September 29. 1653.

All which are preſented to your honours, to do therein as God ſhall direct you, for the good of his people.

RALPH GARDNER.

Tueſday, October 5, 1653.

(N) THE petition of Ralph Gardner, of Northumberland, gentleman, in the behalf of himſelf, and many others, whoſe humble deſires are thereunto annexed, being this day read, the committee conceives it proper, for the committee for trade, and therefore, do recommend the ſame to their conſideration.

ANTHONY ROUS.

At the committee for trade and corporations, ſitting at Whitehall, Oct. 18. 1653.

(o) WHEREAS a petition hath been exhibited, to this committee, by the ſaid Ralph Gardner, of Northumberland, gentleman, in the behalf of himſelf, and many others, complaining of several grievances, they sustain, by the corporation of the town of Newcastle; it is ordered, that the said petition, and complaint, be taken into consideration, by this committee, on tuesday, the 15. of November, next, whereof the mayor and corporation of Newcastle, aforesaid, are to have convenient notice.

SAMUEL WARNER.

(P) The mayor and burgesses of Newcastle, petitioned the committee, beseeching their honours, for a copy of the petition, and paper exhibited, and to grant them fourteen dayes time longer, to make their defence, which their honours granted, but ordered their agents to attend, the 15. day of Nov. to hear the witnesses, on the commonwealths behalf, examined, and to receive, what further should be brought in, by way of charge, against the corporation, by reason, a great trial was had before their honours, with the late farmers of the customes, which took up all that day; the eighteenth day was appointed, for Newcastles businesse, on which day, most of the witnesses were examined, upon this following charge, and proved it, in presence of the corporations agent, and when they were all dismist and gone, the agent desired further time, and the witnesses to be crosse examined, to which the honourable committee replied, that further time they would not give, in a matter of so high concernment, and it was too late to crosse examine the witnesses, he not desiring it, when they were there, and he present, but granted him a copy of the charge.

CHAP.

CHAP. XXVIII.

The heads of the charge, exhibited by Ralph Gardner, of Northumberland, gent. to the committee for trade and corporations, against the mayor, and burgesses of Newcastle, 1653.

(A) THAT the mayor, and burgesses of Newcastle upon Tyne, have, and do imprison artificers, only for their working, upon their lawfull trades. (See stat. 1. 1301.)

(B) That they do force masters of ships, to cut purses, in their open court, for gain to themselves, and imprisons them, if they refuse. See stat. 8. Eliz. 4.

(c) That they force all masters of ships, to swear against themselves, and notwithstanding they have swore the truth, others are called in, to swear against them, which is for a fines sake, which profit accrues to the mayor, burgesses, and witnesse, for their own use.

(D) That they do impose arbitrary fines, so excessively, that without payment, is committed to prison, which said masters are there detained, till the said fine be paid.

(E) That they have robbed people, in their open markets, and in passing through the town, of their goods, alledging foreign bought, and foreign sold. All people, not being free of that town, are reputed foreigners.

(F) That they have imprisoned men, for saving ships from sinking, and detains them till compound; whose poor wives and children, are ready to starve; also keeps them in prison, till they enter into bond, never to work upon their trades again.

(G) That they of that corporation, have taken an oath amongst themselves, not to work with, nor imploy any un-freemen, but to fuppreffe all fuch from working, in that corporation, or the whole river of Tyne.

(H) That they do imprifon poor mafters of fhips, for letting their fhips from finking, and denies bayl.

(I) That they feize of all fuch goods, as any poor mafter doth fave, when their fhips are finking, which is all the poor mafter hath left in the world, to relieve his wife and family, and poor fea-men.

(K) That when any fhip is finking, though feven miles from Newcaftle, none muft help to fave her; but Newcaftle-men muft be fent for, who comes at leifure, befides having his demands, which is exceffive.

(L) That they ingroffe all merchandize, and other dead victual, and provifion, which comes in by fea, and then forces the countries, to give them their own rates, for what they want.

(M) They will not fuffer any provifions to be bought at Shields, or any market to be there, notwithftanding people are often drowned, in going and returning from Newcaftle markets, and alfo, many are ready to ftarve in the winter feafon, by reafon the river is then frozen up, and fo become innavigable.

(N) That they, by ingroffing all corn into their hands, have kept it to fo exceffive rates, that the poor could not buy it, but have been conftrained to eat beafts blood baked, inftead of bread.

(O) That by fuch hoarding up the corn, and the people not able to buy the fame, being fo dear, many country people, were neceffitated to eat dogs and cats, and to kill their poor little coal-horfes for food.

(P) They have hoarded up fo much corn, and keeping it for fuch exceffive gain, that in the very time of fcarcity, and mifery amongft the people, many have been found ftarved to death in holes; hundred bouls of corn were caft into the river, being

fpoyled

spoyled with the rats, and rot: The very swine could not eat it.

(q) That they will not suffer any of the coal owners, in any of the two counties, to sell their own coals, but the owners must either sell their coals, to the free hoast-men, at what price they please, and then all ships must give them their own price, or get none, which makes coals so dear.

(r) That no ship shall be loaden with coals, &c. that will not do, what the mayor and burgesses commands them, by going up the river, seven miles with ballast, to their great losse of time, and hurt of their ships.

(s) That ships have been often ten or fourteen daies, in sailing up and down the river, onely to discharge their ballast, they, for the most part, taking in their loading at Shields. See chap. 32. (c).

(t) That other ships, which have taken in their loading at Shields, with coals and salt, have made their voyage, to London and back, before such ships, which were so compelled to Newcastle, could get ready, and, ordinarily, is the cause of their loss of three voyages in the year, by such compulsions. See chap. 32. (d).

(u) That they force all ships, with materials, brought in by sea, for the absolute use of the salt-works, and coal-works, at and near Shields, to be carryed to Newcastle, and laid out upon their key, though they have no use for the same, and the customs being already paid, and officers at Shields attending; often the boats that fetches them sinks, in returning to Shields. See chap. 50. (c).

(w) That ships have often sunk, in returning empty from Newcastle to Shields, there being nothing to be had at Newcastle, and such ships are onely to take in salt, or coals, at Shields: No salt to be got elsewhere, but at Shields, in that river, and thereabouts. See chap. 29. 30. 32.

(x) That

(x) That they will not tollerate any feaman, though never fo able a pilot, to guide a ftrangers fhip into the river, over Tynemouth-bar, though he be in never fo great diftrefs, but a freeman muft be fent for, from Newcaftle, there being but two at Shields, by means whereof the fhip is often ready to be loft, before any can get feven miles up, and feven miles back again. See chap. 32. (A).

(Y) That they force all fhips, though never fo long, great, or weak, to fail up the river, to caft out their ballaft upon their fhoars, for the gain of eight-pence, for every tun a fhip carries, which is an arbitrary impofition, fee chap. 32. (B.C), it formerly being but four-pence; and one fhip with another, carrys an 100 tun, every voyage, &c. See chap. 29. (C).

(A.B) That they force mafters of fhips, to pay for eighty tun, when indeed they have but forty tun, and fo opprefs the poor mafters, whereby the price of coals muft needs be enhanft. See chap. 44. (A).

(A.F) That they have fpoiled the river, with their ballaft fhoars, by fhips finking in failing up the river, and returning back, their ballaft-fhoars being fo full, and heavy, and hilly, that every fhower of rain, and ftorm of wind doth blow and wafh down the ballaft into the river, befides the weight, in preffing down the walls, to the great prejudice of the commonwealth; by the obftruction of the river, and endangering of fhipping. See chap. 34. (A), 35. (A.B).

(A.G) That by the negligence of the commiffioners, for the river, above three thoufand tuns of ballaft have fallen into the river, in one nights time. See chap. 34. (C). None taken up, &c.

(A.H) That within this twenty years, where twenty fhips of a certain burden could have rid afloat, in moft road-fteads in the river, at a low water mark, now, not above four fhips can ride afloat, &c. See chap. 35. (B).

(A.I) That fhips have made twelve voyages in the year, within this 20 years, when they had liberty, to
caft

caſt their ballaſt at Shields, and now, they make but four or five voyages only, being obſtructed by the mayor, and burgeſſes of Newcaſtle, in compelling the ſhips up the river, ſeven miles, to caſt out their ballaſt, upon their own ſhoars, &c. See chap 32. (D).

(A.K) That they will not ſuffer any ballaſt-ſhoars to be built, at or near the Shields, by reaſon, the owners of the ground will not fell it to them, notwithſtanding there are convenient places, for ſhoars, for above this hundred years to come, without any prejudice to the river, and to the great advantage of the commonwealth. See chap. 29. (C).

(A.L) That they do hinder the ſtock of the publick revenue, above forty thouſand pounds per an. in cuſtoms, *declaro.* See chap. 45. (B.E.F), 32. (D).

(A.M) That they do hinder a trade, all the winter ſeaſon, by reaſon, neither ſhips, nor boats, can paſs up the river, which is often frozen, below the ballaſt-ſhoars, called the Bill-point, and half down the river, it never freezeth lower. See chap. 35. (B).

(A.N) That the mayor, and burgeſſes of Newcaſtle have combined, and made new ordinances amongſt themſelves, that what free hoaſt-men, or filler of coals, ſhall ſell any coals, to ſuch ſhip-maſters, as ſhall caſt any ballaſt at Shields, and not upon their own ballaſt ſhoars, ſhall forfeit and pay, 20l. a time, or lie in priſon, till the ſame be paid. See chap. 43. (D), 30. (D).

(A.O) That all ſuch coals as ſhall be ſold, and not being free of that corporation, ſhall be confiſcated, for the corporations uſe. See 21. chap. (A).

(Some ſay, if what is here alledged, be nothing but the truth, it were pity, but they ſhould receive judgement, according to their reſpective offences, but if it appear otherwiſe, it were pity, but the evidence upon oath, with myſelf, ſhould receive the ſame judgement.)

(A.P) That the mayor and burgeſſes, by having betrayed the truſt, repoſed in them, by king James, in the

the two and twenty articles, for the prefervation of the river of Tyne, have forfeited all that corporations liberties, into the ftates hand, by the exorbitant abufes committed, and negleɛt, in not putting them in execution. See chap. 13. (A), 34. (C).

(A.Q.) All which faid charge was proved upon oath, before the council, at White-hall, 1650, and the committee for trade and corporations, at Whitehall, in November, 1653. And order was given, that Mr. Thomas Skinner, be defired to draw up an act, for a free trade, in that port, and river of Tyne, to prefent to the parliament, fee chap. 54. (which act was intended.) Whether it be confonant to religion, or reafon, that thefe things fo perpetrated, aforefaid, againft the good of a commonwealth, fhould be neglected, and in not being timely regulated, I refer to better judgements.

RALPH GARDNER.

(A.R) Mr. Mark Shafto, Mr. Ralph Jennifon, Mr. Robert Ellifon, Mr. Tho. Bonner, the recorder, and aldermen of Newcaftle, with Mr. John Rufhworth, one Maddifon, and one Michael Bonner, with many more of the burgeffes, appeared at Whitehall, on the 29. of November, being the day appointed, for the town to plead to the charge, they having had the copy of the charge, where the full committee was met, and many parliament-men more, where the petition, the charge, and the defires were read, to the foregoing gentlemen.

(A.S) The corporation, agents, and aldermen, humbly begged ten weeks longer time, by reafon they were not ready, nor prepared to anfwer the charge, for it ftruck at all that was neer, and dear unto them*; and hoped the town would not be furprifed, and that they did conceive Mr. Gardner had fent down that order to affront the town, by reafon it was dropt at the mayors door, by a boy; and that there was a paper, printed by Mr Gardner, which was

* Oppreffion.

was as full of lyes, as words, which did conclude them, and difhearten their witneffes, alfo, that the Scots having tumbled their records, could not draw up an anfwer in fo fhort a time.

(A.T.) In anfwer to the town, it was humbly moved, their honours would give no longer time, by reafon it was the day fet, and agreed upon, that they of the corporation fhould plead, and that it was no new matter infifted upon, but what was debated at that board two years before; the records and judgement, given againft Newcaftle, being in their honours cuftody, and that they were as well able to plead then, as at any other time, and if there were any new matter, it fhould be withdrawn, and was willing to joyn iffue, upon the former judgement, granted two years before, at the fame board.

The towns agents altogether refufed that, and hoped their honours would not infift upon the former judgement, but to give them longer time, they not being ready to plead to the faid charge, nor came prepared, upon the earneft folicitation of the towns agents. The committee told them, that if they would deal clearly and candidly with them, as to give in writing, under their hands, fuch an anfwer to the charge, as they would ftand and fall by, then they would give them their own time, if not, then they would record that fair motion, and that they muft plead, by reafon they appeared, and entred upon a plea, and their work was very fhort, for all that they had to do, was to plead guilty, or not guilty; if guilty, then to make it good by what law they did fuch things, as was laid to their charge, and if not guilty, then it was left to Mr. Gardner to prove his charge, (who indeed had proved all fufficiently) and therefore would give no more day, whatever, then the 13. of December, and Mr. Gardner left free, to bring in what more he had to charge them with. Upon the 12. day of December, the parliament was difmiffed.

But the honourable committee, met in Whitehall, and drew up another report, and figned the fame, againft the corporation of Newcaftle, and would have prefented the fame to his highneffe, the lord protector.

But I conceived to give a narrative was better, though it be large; yet fuch things as are pertinent, might be fooner collected, being put together, and more fatisfactory to all hands, then lying in feveral courts diftractedly; not doubting, but thereby to reap the fruits, according to my labour, I not in the leaft defpairing, and am fatisfied with the change, defiring God to go along with him, in all his highneffe undertakes.

C H A P. XXIX.

DEPOSITIONS.

Ships upon fands, others finking, others funk; boats, and provifions caft away, and people drowned, &c. and others caft into prifon, for faving fhips from finking; all done at Newcaftle, by order of thofe magiftrates; all wreck being given them by charter.

SEE PLATE FIRST, FIGURE FIRST.

* Mr. Fuller.
* Andronicus or the unfortunate politition.

ANDRONICUS* the tyrant, and alfo an heathen king, being overcome with a reluctancy of heart, feeing the miferable condition, poor merchants and fea-men were in, after fhipwreck, (and fhould receive fo bad a reward from people, whom they came to, for help or fhelter) by having their goods feized on, their throats cut, and no relief afforded, by thofe, that got all the fea had caft up for fuccour, they never taking any pains for the fame, made a law, whofoever took a bit of wreck,

Fig. I. page 71.

Fig. II. see page 86.

Published Oct. 1st 1796, by D. Akenhead & Sons, Newcastle upon Tyne

wreck, for their own ufe, fhould be put to death, but that all fhould be preferved for a time, or the worth, for the right owner, and if not looked after by the owner, then for fuch, as were fufferers by fhipwreck, for the future, and the people paid, for their pains in faving of it ; for which law they were cannonized.

Let not tyrants and heathens out-ftrip us in mercy and juftice. This law we want.

(A) Mary Hume, upon her oath, faid, that all fhips and boats, are compelled, by the mayor and burgeffes of Newcaftle, to fail up the river to their ballaft fhoars, and town, with all manner of victuals, which are brought into that river, and will not fuffer any market to be at Shields, which is feven miles from them, and twelve miles from any other market town, in the fame county, and that they compel all people to their markets,* by which means, fhe hath known many ‖ fhips and boats caft away, in the faid river, by ftormy weather. (Read ftat. 27. Ed. 1.*) See chap. 49. (B)*), chap. 10. (s), ‖ 31. (A).

(B) She, the faid Mary, further affirms, that fhe hath known many people drowned, and boats caft away in ftormy weather, in that river, and provifions; and that in or about the year 1650, one William Rea of Shields, was drowned in coming from Newcaftle market; alfo a young gentleman, fon to Mr. Snape, minifter, in Northumberland, was drowned in that river ; both which were found, and buried at Shields, but no coroner* viewed their dead bodies, which fhe hath heard fhould have been done, by Newcaftles coroner, being tyed to it by charter. See chap. 10. (O.P). Alfo William Grays mother in-law, of North Shields, in going to market, was caft away, &c.

MARY HUME.

(c) John

(c) John Mallen, mafter of a fhip, upon his oath, faid, that the mayor and burgeffes of Newcaftle, do deny to load any fhips, nor fuffer any others to load them, with coals, who refufe to fail up that dangerous river feven miles, to caft out ballaft upon their fhoars, which compulfions caufeth the loffe of many fhips,* and veffels in that river, amongft fands, fhelves, and funk fhips, it being merely for the gain of eightpence per tun, of ballaft. See chap. 31. (A.B.), 32. (B)*.

(D) That he, this deponent, was in company with one Mr. James Beats, of Alborough, who was mafter of a new fhip, being compelled to fail up the river, to caft out his ballaft, upon their unlawful ballaft fhoars, and in returning to Shields, to take in her loading of coals, in the middle of the river, his fhip funk, and none durft help to fave her, for fear of being imprifoned, as others were for the like, nor to weigh her up again. See chap. 30. (A).

(E) The free-men came, and required a greater fumme* to weigh her up, then fhe was worth; fo the poor mafter was forced to leave her, upon fmall termes; but foon after, they got her up, and fet her to fea, for their own ufe, which the faid mafter, Beats, might have done the like, if thofe of Newcaftle, would have tollerated the un-freemen to work, who were as well able to perform that fervice. See chap. 30. (F), 36. (A)*, ftat. 2. Ed. 6. 15.*

All wreck is given to them. See chap. 10. 8.

JOHN MALLEN,
THOMAS HEISLEWOOD.

CHAP.

C H A P. XXX.

(A) THOMAS GOSNAL, mafter, affirms, that the mayor and burgeffes of Newcaftle, by compelling all fhips, up that dangerous river of Tyne, feven miles, is the caufe of the loffe of many fhips; and that Mr. Cafon loft his fhip upon the Bill-point, which funk, but by weighing her up again, it coft him near two hundred and fifty pounds, all which might have been faved, if fhips could be tollerated to caft ballaft at Shields. See chap. 25. (B), chap 10. (S), 32. (C.E).

THOMAS GOSNAL.

(B) Edmund Tye, of Ipfwich, fenior, upon his oath, faid, that being with his fhip, laden with coals, riding at anchor, at Shields, with the fleet of fhips, ready to put forth to fea, his fhip funk, by a fad difafter to his undoing, being moft of it his own, and in the time of finking, procured help to fave what goods he could, for relief of himfelf, and feamen, who had faved to the value of one hundred and fifty pound, and fent them on fhoar, to Shields, in the county of Northumberland.* The mayor, and burgeffes of Newcaftle,

(C) Sent down their officers, and feized of all his goods, and fent them to Newcaftle, and carried him, this deponent, to their prifon, and kept him above fix months, becaufe his fhip funk. The goods and fhip, were worth about eleven hundred and fifty pound, and would detain him in prifon, till he did weigh up the faid fhip, who had not wherewithall to relieve himfelf, Exod. 22. 21. notwithftanding they were certified fo much, under the bayliffs hands, and town feal of Ipfwich, and had continued him longer, if he had not procured a habeas corpus, for his removal, to London. See chap. 25. (B), 10. (S), ftat.

(s), ſtat. 3. Edw. 1. 15. 34. 14. Rich. 2. 9. 23. Hen. 6. 10.

EDMUND TYE.

(D) Thomas Heiſlewood, of London, maſter of a ſhip, upon his oath, ſaid, having taken in his ſhips loading of coals, in the river of Tyne, was putting forth to ſea, with the fleet, but by a ſtorm was caſt aſhoar, neer Tinmouth-bar, and in great danger of their lives, which were on board of the ſaid ſhip, and was conſtrained to caſt his coals into the ſea, and thereby got his ſhip to Shields, where ſhe lay like a wreck, the water having free paſſage in and out.

(E) He, this deponent got on ſhoar, and repaired to one —— Collier, a free carpenter of Newcaſtle, deſiring him to mend his ſhip, and, for haſtes ſake, he would procure thirty or forty of his neighbours, maſters of ſhips carpenters, to help him, but the ſaid free carpenter replied, that he had taken an * oath in Newcaſtle, with their company, neither to work with any unfree carpenter, nor to ſet any on work, by which means, he, this deponent, was conſtrained to patch up his ſhip, with his ſingle carpenter, and adventure to London, to get her upon the ſtock, where he, and his company were in great hazard of their lives, and loſſe of the ſhip. See chap. 10. (s), ſee ſtat. 19. Hen. 7. 7. (2. Edw. 6. 15.*)

THO. HEISLEWOOD.

* If all maſters ſhould be thus tyed to buy all things of them, judge of the conſequence.

(F) Henry Harriſon, maſter, upon his oath, ſaid, that his ſhip was laden with corn; coming in at Tinmouth-bar, loſt her rudder, or ſteerer of his ſhip; he, this deponent, deſired another, of a free-man of Newcaſtle, who would not furniſh him, under forty ſhillings,* but this deponent got a good one, of an un-freeman, one Thomas Cliffe, of Shields, carpenter. See chap. 29. (E), 36. (A), for 6s. 8d.

HENRY HARRISON.

CHAP.

CHAP. XXXI.

(A) MICHAEL BONNER, of Newcaftle, merchant, and water-fergeant, in Janu. 1649, being examined upon oath,* at Gates-head, by vertue of a commiffion, in a caufe depending in the exchequer, between the mayor and burgeffes, complainants, and Thomas Cliffe, defendant, faid, that a fhip, called the Adventure, of Ipfwich, which was funk in the year 1646, (Mr. Thomas Cafon being mafter;) one other fhip, called the Providence, of London, (Humphrey Harrifon, of London, being mafter,) which funk in the year 1649; one other fhip, called the Refuge, of Ipfwich, funk in October, 1649 (Mr. Edmund Tye, being mafter;) another fhip, called the Henrietta Maria, funk in the year 1644; all which fhips were weighed out of the river of Tyne, at the fole charge of the mayor, and burgeffes of Newcaftle.

MICHAEL BONNER.

Some calls this depofition perjury,* but I refer it to the judgement of the reader, that reads the following depofition, which proves, that moft of the abovefaid fhips lye funk, and did, three years after the depofition. See ftat. 5. Eliz. 9.*

(B) Cap. George Phillips, of London, upon his oath, faid, that there lyes feveral fhips funk in the river of Tyne, between Sparhawk and Heborn Steath, namely, the Adventure,* of London, Humphrey Harrifon, of Sunderland, late mafter, funk in, or about the year 1649; one other fhip, called the Refuge, of Ipfwich, funk in October, 1649, at Shields, (Edmund Tye, the late mafter;) one other fhip, called the Henrietta Maria, funk in the river, in, or about 1644; and one other in the fouth road, late belonging to Mr. Bulman; and alfo, one other fhip, belonging to a fcotch-man, lyes funk neer unto the low lights; and that the chiefe caufe of fhips finking in
that

that river is, by being compelled, by the mayor, and burgeffes of Newcaftle, to fail up that dangerous river, to caft ballaft upon their unlawful ballaft fhoars, for the gain of eightpence, for every tun, fo caft out.

GEORGE PHILLIPS, AND
THO. HESILWOOD, PROVE THE LIKE.

CHAP. XXXII.

(A) GAWEN POTS affirms, that no ftrangers fhip whatever, though fhe be in never fuch great diftreffe, and finking, muft be pylotted into the river, by any other fea-man, then a freeman of Newcaftle: In the intrim, one is fent for, (being fixteen miles forward and backward) often, either fhe is loft, or driven by ftorm away.

MANY OTHERS PROVED THE LIKE.

(B) Jeremiah Low, mafter of a fhip, upon his oath, 1650, faid, that the mayor and burgeffes of Newcaftle, compelling all fhips up the river, to their ballaftfhoars, amongft the dangerous fands, fhelves, and funk fhips, is the caufe of much harm, and loffe of many fhips, and loffe of many voyages in the year, befides loffe to the ftate, and fpoyl of the river; it onely being done for the lucre of eight pence, for every tun of ballaft, to fome private perfons, which brings them in many thoufands of pounds in the year, and that there are many funk fhips in the river, between Sparhawk and Hebourn Steath. See chap. 29. (c).

JEREMIAH LAW, MR. PHILLIPS,
MR. HESILWOOD, PROVE THE LIKE.

(c) John Mallen, mafter of a fhip, upon his oath, faid, that by the mayor and burgeffes compelling
fhips

ships up the river, to their ballaft-shoars, with their ballaft, was the caufe of Mr. Tye, and Mr. Morfes two ships running on the fands, neer Jarrow, where they were both in great danger of being loft.

Mr. Yaxleys ship in a condition of finking, but three unfree carpenters being ready, faved her. Mr. John Willey in the like condition.

Capt. George Phillips was fourteen dayes, in getting up and down to Shields, by which means, much damage is done to their ships, and loffe of feveral voyages, and trade is obftructed.

> Capt. GEO. PHILIPS, Mr. HESILWOOD, Mr. CASON, Mr. MORS, Mr. YAXLY, and Mr. WILLEY, prove the like.

(D) Mr. Keeble, mafter of a ship, proves, that himfelf, with many other mafters of ships, namely, Mr. Wright, &c. have made twelve voyages in the year, when they caft ballaft at Shields, within thefe twenty yeers, and doubts not, but by Gods bleffing, to make as many again, if the ships be allowed to caft ballaft there, which may be done without hurt to the river, and more fafety to ships, and a great revenew to the publick; whereas now, being compelled up to Newcaftle shoars, which hath fpoiled the river, they cannot make above four, five, or fix voyages in the year, at moft, which is many thoufand pounds, per annum, loffe to the ftate, in cuftome.

KEEBLE.

(E) Henry Robinfon, upon his oath, faid, that being compelled, by the mayor and burgeffes, up the river to their ballaft-shoars, his ship fet upon a fand, and broke her keelfon, to his great damage, and loffe of voyage; and that Mr. Cafon his ship, fet upon the point of the Bill, and overfet, which coft him two hundred and forty pound, the recovering of her again, befides the loffe of voyage.

> THOMAS GOSNAL, proves the like.

M CHAP.

CHAP. XXXIII.

(A) THOMAS CLIFFE, upon his oath, said, that in April, 1646, Arthur Lyme, master of a ship, being in the river of Tyne, his ship in great distress and danger of sinking, obtained the present help of three ship carpenters, which were ready at hand, to save his ship from sinking; and because they were not freemen, the mayor and burgesses of Newcastle, sent down several carpenters, belonging to Newcastle, to force them from work, and carried them away to prison, with the said master, for setting them on work, no tryall at law was had, or other offence committed.

THO. CLIFFE.

CHAP. XXXIV.

(A) ———— BIGS, upon his oath, said, that all the ground,* on both sides of the river of Tyne, to a full sea-mark, is the right of the town of Newcastle, and belongs onely to the mayor and burgesses, all the way from Sparhawk to Headwin streams, and that he knoweth the same, by reason he hath seen often the water-sergeant of Newcastle, (by name Charles Mitford) arrest men, both masters and others. This deposition was taken in behalf of Newcastle, at Gates-head, in Jan. 1649, in the suit, between the town and Cliffe, and remains in the exchequer.

———— BIGS.

Some calls this also perjury, but it is left to the judgement of the reader, in reading the next deposition. See chap. 18. (D.F.), stat. 5. Eliz. 9.*

(B) William

(b) William Gibſon, of Newcaſtle, merchant, in Jan. 1649, at Gates-head, upon his oath, ſaid, that the ground, on both ſides of the river of Tyne, from Sparhawk to Headwin ſtreams, from a low water-mark, was not belonging to the town, nor mayor and burgeſſes of Newcaſtle, but to the reſpective owners, in each county, adjoyning on the river, and that he knew the ſame, by reaſon of former trials, and ſo adjudged; and that the town had only the arreſting upon the water, but not upon the land. See chap. 20.

WILLIAM GIBSON.

(c) Thomas Horth, of London, merchant, upon his oath, ſaid, that he had known the river of Tyne, above five and twenty yeers ; and that by reaſon of the mayor, and burgeſſes of Newcaſtle, compelling all ſhips with ballaſt, to ſail up the river, ſeven miles, to unload their ballaſt, and out of keels, upon their own ſhoars, by ballaſt, and other rubbiſh falling in, hath ſpoyled three parts of the river;* whereas within this twenty yeers, twenty ſhips of the burden of two hundred tuns a piece, could have rid a float, in moſt road-ſteads in that river, ‖ and now, not above four or five, at a low water-mark, by reaſon they have ſo little ground, that it is ſo over full, and hilly with the ballaſt, that the winds and rains, every time, doth waſh and blow great quantities off, into the river ; and that in one night, the ſhoar called the Bill-ballaſt-key, brake down, and, at leaſt, three thouſand tun of ballaſt, ſand, gravel, and ſtones, fell down into the river,* and they never knew any taken up.

* Neither will the mayor and burgeſſes ſuffer the owners of grounds, adjoyning to the river, to a low water mark, to build any wharfs, keys, or ballaſt-ſhoars, though more convenient then any are, and would ſerve for many years, without any prejudice to the river, to unlade all ballaſt at; neither will

they, the said owners, fell their grounds to the said magistrates, to be inslaved, by which means the river is spoyled. See stat 34. Hen. 8, 9. * 30. Ed. 1. ‖ See chap. 12. (6.) 14. (B.)

    Thomas Horth, George Philips, and
    Tho. Hasilwood, prove the like.

CHAP. XXXV.

(A) GEORGE PHILIPS, captain, master of a ship, of London, upon his oath, said, that the mayor, and burgesses of Newcastle, is the cause, of hindring a trade for coals, salt, &c. the greatest part of the winter season, to the great impoverishing of the two counties, Northumberland, and Durham, out of which all coals, salt, &c. comes, (none being to be had, nor ever was in Newcastle) by reason the aforesaid mayor, and burgesses having the pre-emption, and will not let the right inheritors sell their own coals, to any ships; (B) nor suffer any of the owners to build ballast-shoars, upon their own land, except they will sell it them; many of which places, neer unto the Shields, is far more convenient, then any of those unlawful shoars, belonging to themselves, at, or neer Newcastle, in the highest part of the river, which hath so much spoyled the said river, especially a place called the Pace-sand, that it is the spoyl of many ships, in sayling up and down, to cast out ballast, and to take in coals. (C) That it must be a good neap tyde, that there is above ten foot, and a half, at high water, and most ships draw twelve foot; also, where there hath lately been ten foot at low water, in a place called the Bill, there is not now above eight foot, occasioned by the sand, and ballast falling off the towns ballast-shoars; (D) and

and that the river, in the winter, is often frozen, below the towns ballaſt ſhoars, at the Bill, (but never lower) that no ſhips can get up to unlade their ballaſt, and take in coals, ſalt. &c. all ſalt being made at Shields where the river is never frozen; but all ſhips reſtrained from caſting ballaſt there, though there be more convenient places, and would ſerve all ſhips, to caſt their ballaſt, for above fourſcore years, without any hurt to the river, or ſhipping, (F) and cauſe them to make more voyages in the year.

  JOHN MORS, WALTER KEEBLE, JAMES SHRIVE, THOMAS HESILWOOD, ROB. SWALLOW, GEORGE HILL, JOHN KEEBLE, HENRY HARRISON, and many other maſters of ſhips, prove the like.

(B) Thomas Haſilwood, of London, maſter of a ſhip, upon his oath, ſaid, that all the ballaſt-ſhoars above the Bill-reach, have been the ſpoyl, and ruine of the river of Tyne, and doth believe, that if no care be taken ſpeedily therein, there will be no navigable river, to the utter impoveriſhing of thoſe counties, and a great prejudice of the whole nation, the greateſt part of navigation, in that river being ſpoyled, as appears in moſt road-ſteads, in the ſaid river of Tyne, what with the ballaſt falling in, and ſhips ſunk, that when, as within theſe twenty years, twenty ſhips of the burden of two hundred tuns, could have rid afloat at low water, at St. Lawrence road-ſtead, now not above three ſhips of the ſame burthen; at the Hands and Dents hole road-ſteads, where twenty ſhips of the ſame burthen, now not above eight can ride afloat; at St. Anthonies, where twenty of the ſame burthen, now, not above three can ride afloat; at the Bill road-ſtead, where twenty of the ſame burthen might have rid, now not above ſix; at the North road-ſtead, where twenty ſhips of the ſame burthen could have rid afloat, now not above four; and at the South road-ſtead, where twelve
            ſhips

ships of the same burthen could have rid afloat, at low water, now not above three can ride; (B) and that within these few years, when ships did cast ballast at Shields, without the molestation of the mayor and burgesses, ships made ten or twelve voyages in the yeer, whereas now, they can make but four or five voyages. See stat. 34. Hen. 8. 9. 23. Hen. 8. 5.

> THO. HASILWOOD, ROB. YAXLEY, GEORGE PHILIPS, WALTER KEEBLE, and HENRY HARRISON, with many more masters of ships, prove the like.

CHAP. XXXVI.

A. *John Hall*, B. *Ann Wallice*, C. *Thomas Rutter*, D. *Ann Cliff*, E. *Free Carpenter*, F. *Cliffs man*.

(SEE PLATE I. FIG. 2.)

(A) HENRY HARRISON, master of a ship, upon his oath, said, that in April, 1646, a ship sailing into Tinmouth haven, by storm, was cast upon the rock, near Tinmouth castle; the master got ashoar with all expedition, and obtained the present help of an antient ship-carpenter, by name, Thomas Cliff, of North-Shields, with three of his men, to save the said ship from perishing, which ship had been quite lost, if the said master should have run to Newcastle, to have agreed with the free carpenters, whose excessive rates* and demands, often surmounts the value of the ship in distress, and their tediousness, in coming and going that distance, that often the ships in distress are quite lost.

(B) The

(B) The said Cliff, and his men, saved the ship, and got her off, and brought her to the lower end of the North Shields, and laid her upon the sands to mend her, where the three carpenters were at work, and Ann, the wife of Thomas Cliff, and Ann Wallice, his daughter, standing, (to see their servants work) near unto the ship.

(C) The mayor, and burgesses of Newcastle, sent Thomas Rutter, and John Hall, two sergeants, with Thomas Otway, Richard Toderick, and other free carpenters of Newcastle, to Shields, to seize upon all the aforesaid workmen, for daring to save any ship from sinking, in that river, with command to carry them to prison.

(D) The two women seeing their servants trailing away, railed against their evil practices, for which, Thomas Rutter, with a club, by several blows upon Ann Cliffs body, and head, knockt her down to the ground; the other sergeant, John Hall, by several blows, with a rule or truncheon, broke Ann Wallice her arme, and then perceiving souldiers coming from Tynmouth castle, both the said sergeants fled to Newcastle, where they were protected from the hand of justice.

(E) The said Ann Cliff was taken up, carried home, got to bed, and in a few weeks dyed* thereon, for which the said Rutter was indited, and found by the jury, guilty, yet did not suffer. The said woman required her friends, as they would answer it at the last day, they should require her blood at the hands of Rutter, he being her death. The poor men kept in prison,* and Cliff kept in suit at law, for his working, by Newcastle, and his men, and they forced to give bond never to work again. See chap. 25. (B), 29. (E), 30. (F), 1. Edw. 6. 12*.

HENRY HARRISON, THOMAS CLIFF, AND
ELEANOR LOUNSDALE, ALL PROVE THE LIKE.

CHAP.

CHAP. XXXVII.

(A) THOMAS SALKIELD, gent. upon his oath, said, that he, being at Shields, in the county of Northumberland, upon the two and twentieth day of May, 1653, saw a great number of men, belonging to Newcastle, with swords drawn, and pistols cockt, who invironed a gentleman, who was peaceably in his house, and shot at some of the said gentlemans servants, and beat his wife, and much blood was spilt, they pretending they came by warrant, and produced a warrant from the mayor, Mr. William Dawson, Mr. John Butler, sheriff of Newcastle, to take him and carry him away to prison, under pretence of debt; but the sea-men got ashoar, fell upon the said Newcastle-men, wounded and disarmed them, and relieved the said gentleman. See stat. 2. Edw. 3. 3. 4. Rich. 2. 37. Hen. 6.

THO. SALKIELD, LETTICE HUME, MARY HUME, AND MANY OTHERS, PROVE THE SAME.

(B) Thomas Salkield, gent. upon his oath, said, he knew a gentleman cast into Newcastle prison, upon a bare arrest, in August, 1652, and laid actions upwards of nine hundred pounds, where twenty pound could not be recovered; and kept him lockt up in a prison, from all comforts, in a tower, above 36 foot high, being forced to evacuate in the same room he lay, and eat his meat, by reason he was locked from the house of easement.

(C) He offered good bayl, free-men of Newcastle, who were accepted, and entered in the book, and two daies after rased out again, and he still kept there. He desired to be admitted to defend his own cause, in their court, but they refused it.

(D) Desired to go with a keeper to counsel, which was also denied; his friends and servants often not admitted to come to him.

(E) Proffered

(E) Proffered good bond to be a true prisoner, to the end he might have the benefit of the fresh aire, for preservation of his health, but at the goalers house; which the sheriff granted, at the first, but presently after refused, saying, that the mayor, aldermen, and himself had a meeting, and resolved, he should have no liberty, being an enemy against their privileges.

(G) The said gentleman offered them, that what any could recover against him by law, they should have it without law.

(H) Constrained to drink the goalers beer, not fit for mens bodies.

(I) No tryal ever against him; they disobeyed two or three habeas corpusses, which the sheriff received, and his fee, and was proffered to have their charges born, but never returned them.

(K) Refused substantial bond, to appear at London, before the judges, and after five months imprisonment, he brake prison, in February following.

(L) And he further affirms, that upon the third of February, 1652, one John Cuthbertson, being imprisoned, upon an action of 5l. debt, but no tryal ever had against him, for the same, was upon this gentlemans getting away, cast into the dungeon, by the command of the magistrates of Newcastle, where they laid fetters of iron upon him, to force a confession from him, whether he did not help the said gentleman out; where he lay upon the cold earth, without either bed, straw, or any other thing to keep him warm, or firing, and fed him onely with bread and water, and fused comfortable subsistance to be brought unto him.

(M) The poor man being not worth, in the whole world, forty shillings, and two children a begging, and himself kept in prison, after this impression, begging for food.

(N) And that he was certainly informed; that some of the officers of Newcastle, had counterfeited a letter, and set the gentlemans name to it, and read it to the said.

said prisoner, thereby perswading him to confess he helped him out of prison. See stat. 23. Hen. 6. 10. 1. Edw. 1. 15. See chap. 41.

Thomas Salkeild.

Hornes Mirror saith, it is an abuse, that prisoners be charged with irons, before they be attainted, cap. 8. sect. 1. 2 Edw. 3. 10. 1. Edw. 3. 10.

Bracton saith, to lay a man in chains is against the law, for a prison is to keep, not to punish.

And it is commanded by the law, that neither felon, nor trespasser be punished, nor tormented, in prison, fo. 11. 17.

Fleta saith, it is lawful for sheriffs to keep prisoners in prison, but not to punish them, but keep them, &c. 33. Hen. 1. P. Inst. 54. See chap. 41. (A).

CHAP. XXXVIII.

(A) RALPH TAYLER, publick notary, and steward to the carpenters of Newcastle, upon his oath, at Gateshead, in January, 1649, said, that the mayor and burgesses of Newcastle, did sue,* imprison,* and fine,* Robert Johnson, Alexander Hearon, and William Portice, of the town of Gateshead; John Hubbert, of South-Shields, and John Readhead, only for working upon ships, in the river of Tyne, being carpenters, and made them to pay their fines, imposed upon them, by the mayor and burgesses. See stat. 2. Edw. 3. 6. 28. Edw. 3. 3.* 9. Hen. 3. 29.* 43. Eliz. 2.*

Ralph Tayler, and Mich. Bonner, prove the like.

(B) Michael Bonner, merchant, and water-sergeant of Newcastle, at the same time, upon his oath, said, that the mayor and burgesses of Newcastle, arrested and

and imprifoned, and fet a fine, upon one John Hardcaftle, a carpenter, for working upon a fhip, in the river of Tyne, he not being a freeman of that corporation, and made him enter into a bond of 100l. in May, 1648, never to work upon his trade again, and made him pay his fine.
MICHAEL BONNER.

(c) John Hall, upon his oath, faid, that the mayor, and burgeffes of Newcaftle, did arreft, imprifon, fined, fued, and forced bonds, from one Richard Tayler, Henry Atchefon, and Robert Lambert, fmiths, whofe wives and families inhabits, at North-Shields, in the county of Northumberland, and Thomas Brocket, of Gatefhead, in the county of Durham, fmith, for no other offence than for working upon their lawfull trades, where they dwell; Tayler and Brocket ftood out fuit, Atchefon entered into bond, never to work upon his trade, to the fhips on the the river, and Lambert kept in prifon, till almoft ftarved,* his wife and fix fmall children begging for food. See ftat. 9. Hen. 3. 29.* 43 Eliz. 2.
JOHN HALL.

(D) Ralph Bowes, of Newcaftle, late burgefs, but disfranchized, upon his oath, faid, in January, 1649, that, formerly, he had feen an antient writing, belonging to the mayor, and burgeffes of Newcaftle, purporting, that it was unlawful for any tradefmen to work, or live in any port, adjoyning to the river of Tyne, but onely at the town aforefaid, and that the mayor and burgeffes, have had the punifhing of all fuch as did work, as alfo the correction thereof, in that port, &c.
RALPH BOWES.

It is pitty this gentleman is not reftored to his freedom again, for this his great difcovery. Surely this faid writing was made by the corporation themfelves, it was fo confciencioufly drawn, it having fo little regard to the weal of the publick.

CHAP. XXXIX.

D. *The mayor and witnesses.* C. *The master swearing.* A. *The master cutting a purse.* B. *The clarks telling the mony. To swear against themselves, to be imprisoned, to cut a purse, to pay a fine, are four punishments for one offence.*

(SEE PLATE 2. FIG. 1.)

(A) THOMAS HASILWOOD, of London, master of a ship, upon his oath, said, that all masters of ships, which sayleth into the river of Tyne, for coals, salt, &c. the mayor, and burgesses of Newcastle, compels them to * swear against themselves, whether they did not cast ballast at sea, between Sowter and Hartly, or within fourteen fathom water, to the hurt of the said river of Tyne, and when the said master hath sworn the truth, that he did not, then a poor drunken filher-man, or other, is called into the town chamber, and maketh oath, that the master did cast ballast, when in truth he did not, he having part of the fine for the same.

(B) Then the masters oath is invalid, and laid aside,* and forthwith is commanded to pay a fine of five pounds, or else to cut a purse, which hangs up in the town-chamber, with sand and money in it, and so much as is therein, he must pay, or is sent to prison, and there to lye till he doth pay it. See chap. 14, (F)* 12. 5. 17. k. Charles, (19. Hen. 7. 7.).

THO. HASILWOOD, JOHN LOCKWOOD, and SAM. JAMES, masters of ships, prove the like. . Read these statutes.

(C) Thomas Bradford, of Lyn, affirms, that in, or about the year, 1652, the mayor, and burgesses of Newcastle, compelled one Richard Nesling, master of a ship,

Plate II. Fig. I. page 92.

Fig. II. See page 106.

Published Oct 1st 1796 by D. Akenhead & Sons, Newcastle upon Tyne

a ſhip, to cut a purſe,* hanging up in the town-chamber, with monies in it, and paid money for ſo doing. See chap. 12. (5) ſtat. 8. Eliz. 4.*

THO. BRADFORD.

(D) In Spain, if any perſon do inform againſt another, let the ſuggeſtion be what it will, and the information never ſo falſe, the party informed againſt, is ſent to priſon, and there kept, till he do confeſs that it is truth, and thereupon is lead to the ſtake, and executed.

(E) The heathen kings, when they condemn a perſon, to dye for any offence, firſt ſends him a pair of ſcales, and a weight; if the malefactor ſends him ſo much gold, as the weight weigheth, is ſaved, otherwiſe not.

(F) The Star-chamber practice was to put a man to his oath, to betray himſelf, and confeſſe as much as he pleaſed, and then other witneſſes were brought in againſt him, as that of the lord Bucan, and the warden of the Fleet, upon a complaint made againſt the warden, in the Star-chamber, &c. See ſtat. 17. Carol.

CHAP. XL.

(A) JOHN HARRISON, of London, upon his oath, ſaid, that all maſters of ſhips, belonging to the coal trade, at Newcaſtle, are compelled to ſwear how many coals, and chaldrons, they have aboard their ſhips, at Newcaſtle, when they are loaden, which is impoſſible to ſwear, by reaſon they buy their coals by weight, and often the maſters occaſions draws them aſide, ſo are not then aboard, when the coals are ſhipped, but truſts to his,

his, or their mates; and often the coal boat, hath much water, which weighs heavy, alfo great ftore of flates, and other rubbifh; and often the fhips are loaden in the night, fo that this oath, is a great vexation to their fpirits, and difquieting thereof; and conceives that never a time, a mafter fwears, but he is perjured, and often deceived by the keelsmen in the nayles.

Capt. JAMES GREENWAY, proves the like.

(B) The oath, *ex officio*. No man is bound by the law of God, or laws of the land of England, to betray himfelf, *in criminalibus, licet in contractibus*, not in criminal offences, but in contracts and bargains, it may be whether he did make the contract or bargain, in queftion, but never ufed to a malefactor, for if witneffes do not come in againft him, he is cleared by law, and not put to his oath, to accufe himfelf.

(c) Many are conftrained to take an oath, *de rebus ignotis*, to anfwer to they know not to what, but Gods command is, fwear not at all.

(D) Query, whether it be lawful for one to fwear, being forced?

(E) The anfwer. Magiftrates may impofe an oath, with thefe three limitations; firft, if the thing be weighty; fecondly, if otherwife it cannot be known; thirdly, if it be not a fnare to catch a mans felf, or trick to make him accufe himfelf; fecondly, magiftrates fhould be very wary, how they inforce, or conftrain men to fwear, becaufe they often thereby add fuel unto the fire of Gods wrath, by making men forfwear themfelves, and therefore it were better to loofe the thing in queftion, than hazard the lofs of a brothers foul, by making him perjure himfelf. Paul would rather chufe never to eat flefh, than to offend his weak brother.

(G) If ye believe him when he fwears, why not upon a folemn proteftation? It fhould be confidered,

whether

whether such as is to be put to his oath, fears God, then he dares no more lye than forswear himself, and if he fear not God, how will he fear to forswear himself?

(H) The practice in Newcastle is worse, for notwithstanding a man is put to his oath, against himself, it will not stand, but another is called in, to swear point blanck against what he had sworn.

CHAP. XLI.

(A) WILLIAM LING, master of a ship, of Ipswich, upon his oath, said, that Henry Truelove, master of a ship, with himself, did cast their ballast, at Shields, upon a sufficient shoar, without any harm to the river, for which, (B) the mayor, and burgesses of Newcastle, arrested them both, and detained them, till they did pay ten pounds fine, for this offence, as they called it.

(c) He, this deponent, with Mr. Truelove, tendered sufficient bail, freemen*, to answer the great council, or the common law, for any thing that they had done; this they could not deny by their power, P. 17. N. 7. (D) but the mayor and aldermen, sharply reproved the bondsmen, for daring to offer themselves as bail, and told to him, this deponent, and Mr. Truelove, that for a great council there was none, and for the common law, that they had within themselves, and needed not to yeeld to any other court, and that to prison they should go, and lye and rot, till they had paid the fine. P. 17. N. 7.

And then cast them both, into their stinking common goal, where onely a wall parted them, and such as had the plague, where they lay, in that sad and miserable condition, in hazard of their lives, (G) and was forced to pay the said ten pounds, and all
charges,

charges, besides the loss of their voyage, which amounted to above 80l. to their owners. (H)* There was no tryal at law, nor any other offence committed, but they could get no right, by reason they were to have the fines, and being judges, jurors, and witnesses, in their own court, and for their own benefits. See stat. 11. R. 2. 9. (A), see chap. 18. (C), 23. Hen. 6. 10. See chap. 37. (D), 28. Edw. 3. 3. (F), 1. Rich. 2. 13. 99. (G), 1. Ed. 3. 15. (C).

WILLIAM LING, and HENRY TRUELOVE,
swears the like.

(B) Joseph Priestly, with John Walker, the minister of Jarrow, and twelve more, upon a tryal, at Durham assizes, between the dean and chapters, plaintiffs, against Thomas Talbot, and Richard Allen, gent. concerning the right of Jarrow* Slike, which by verdict was given to the defendants, upon their oathes, said, that they knew Jarrow Slike, by estimation three hundred acres, where a wall was building, to have it a ballast-shoar, for the good of ships and river, 22. Feb. 1638, by Ling and Truelove, and that the ballast which was cast thereon, was cast without any prejudice to the river, and there lay safe and sad, and that neither the wind could ever blow it off, nor the rain, nor waves could wash it into the river. See chap. 34. (A.D).*

JOSEPH PRIESTLY, JOHN WALKER.

How long will yee give wrong judgement, to accept the persons of the ungodly? Psa. 82. 2.

CHAP.

C H A P. XLII.

(A) CAPTAIN ROBERT WYARD, of London, upon his oath, faid, that he, with his fhip, being in the river of Tyne, at Newcaftle, in Nov. 1649, where one of his fhips company (it feems) did caft two or three ftraw mats, out of one of his fhips port-holes, yet, to this deponents unknowledge, which could do no harm to the river, by reafon of its fwiming to fea*; but one Edward Green, and one ——— Wilkinfon, two free-men of Newcaftle, ftanding a quarter of a mile from the fhip, upon the land, made oath, at Newcaftle, that this deponent caft out ballaft into the river, to the prejudice thereof.

* It could do no harm to the river, other than endanger the choaking of the fifh.

(B) Whereupon the mayor, and burgeffes of Newcaftle feized him, and fined him twenty pounds‖ for the fame, and conftrained him to pay ten pound of it, and ten pound to Green, and eight pounds to Wilkinfon, and twenty four pounds more the fuit coft him, being fined by them, for faying they were forfworn, to fay he caft ballaft into the river, when he neither did, nor was out of his cabin when the mats were caft in.

‖ Yet the tol. did not cleanfe the river thereof.

ROBERT WYARD. *1.Tim.6.10.

(C) And further faith, that the mayor and burgeffes, were plaintiffs, judges, jurors, and witneffes in this caufe, of their own fines. See chap. 11. (E), ftat. 5. Eliz. 9.

If thefe men be fined fo high, for fo fmall an offence, and that ignorantly, what muft thofe men that have offended arrogantly and knowingly, a thoufand times more? Thomas Peach, mafter of the Ann Speedwel, of Ipfwich, who, by ftorm, was caft upon the rocks, near Tinmouth caftle, and for cafting his baliaft over-board, to fave his fhip, was fined by the mayor and burgeffes.

O
Mr.

Mr. James Talbot, for his men sweeping the bins of his ship, where there could not lie above one shovel full of ballast, was fined five pounds, and laid it down; some they took, and some they returned to him again.

CHAP. XLIII.

(A) NICHOLAS PYE, of London, creup, upon his oath, said, that Mr. Thomas Partridge, of Gateshead, master, being loaded at Newcastle, by Thomas Read, Fitter, with bad and unmerchantable coals, which he had sold for good coals, to Mr. Clark, of London, and M. Otridge, M. Godfrey, M. Harrison, and others, at the rate of 31l. the score, but proving so bad, that he was threatened to be sued, by the said gentlemen that bought them, and was constrained to compound for the same, and lost 6l. in every score, and that he hath known much bad coals, which the freemen of Newcastle forceth masters of ships to take, to the great loss on all hands.

NICHOLAS PYE.

Pray look into the tenth year of king James, what punishment hath been for the same, formerly.

The said Thomas Read, did give 20l. as part of satisfaction, to the said Mr. Tho. Partridge, the master, and in consideration of his great wrong, &c.

(B) Captain Gregory Butler, captain of a man of war, for the parliament, upon his oath, said, that in April, 1650, he, this deponent, wanting some ballast for his ships use, being at Shields, required a master of a ship, of Yarmouth, to cast his ballast into his ship, for the states use, which the said master did

did with much care, and no prejudice to the river, (c) for which the mayor, and burgesses of Newcastle, refused to suffer any coals to be laid on board of his ship, till he paid 5l. fine, for this contempt, and forced him to pay a fine, and to pay eight pence, for every tun of ballast (besides) computing it to 48 tun, and then, and not before, he could get any coals. See chap. 44.

GREGORY BUTLER.

Thomas Partridge, master, affirms, that Mr. alderman Samuel Rawling, forced him to pay for 80 tuns of ballast, when he carryed but 42 tun. Every freeman pays fix pence the tun, and un-freeman pays eight pence. There is no warrant to demand any such sum.

THOMAS PARTRIDGE.

(D) Richard Leaver, of Ipswich, master of a ship, upon his oath, said, that for his casting out ballast, at Shields, upon a more convenient shoar, than any was at Newcastle, and without any hurt to the river, went to Newcastle, to the coal fitter, to be laden, but could get none, by reason of a combination of the free hoast-men, who had made a new ordinance* amongst themselves, in the free hoast-mens court, that who should dare to sell a coal to any such master of a ship, as did not cast ballast upon the town shoars, should forfeit twenty pound a time.

(E) Upon which, this deponent waited above ten dayes, and could not get coals for money, but at last prevailed, with one of the fitters of coals at Newcastle, by promising him to save him harmlesse, and he would load him, which was done, for which the said mayor and burgesses, cast the said fitter into prison, where he lay, till a fine of five pound was paid for his ransome, with other charges, which he, this deponent, was forced to pay, besides losse of his voyage. This was without any triall at law, &c. (See 19. Hen. 7. 7.*) 28. Ed. 3. 3.

RICH. LEAVER.

CHAP. XLIV.

(A) RICH. LEAVER, of Ipswich, master of a ship, upon his oath, said, that for the only gain and advantage of some aldermen, and a few other private persons, of the town of Newcastle, no masters of ships can be tollerated to cast ballast, in any part, but at their ballast-shoars, which is unlawful, and very prejudicial to the river and trade, and must often pay for eighty tun of ballast,* when indeed there is but forty to be paid for, (B) and do hinder all coals from being sold, to any ship which do cast ballast at Shields, upon as sufficient shoars, and better than the other, both for the good of the river, and lesse hurt to ships, and more voyages made in the year; (C) also, that the mayor and burgesses, do prohibit all the coal-owners, in both counties of Northumberland, and Durham, for selling their own coals, it tending to the said owners utter undoing, and the cause of many voyages lost in the year, to the great prejudice of the poor, and much losse to the state, (D) and that there is more convenient places, to build ballast-shoars, which will last, for hundreds of years, without hurt to the river, at, and neer Shields, then where they are at present. See chap. 43. See the following deposition.

RICHARD LEAVER.

CAPT. BUTLER, SAMUEL JAMES, CAPT. PHILIPS, and JEREMIAH LOW, proves the like.

(E) Thomas Cartwright, of Lyn, merchant, upon his oath, said, that by reason all coals are ingrossed, and sold by the free-men, the mayor, and burgesses of Newcastle, onely tends to the great impoverishment of the coal owners of the two counties, where all the coals are.

(F) Also,

(F) Alfo, that it is the caufe of the high and exceffive rates of coals, at London, and fea-coafts, and lofe to the mafters, feveral voyages in the year.

(G) And to the ftate likewife, in cuftomes of the three fhillings per chalder.

(H) And that he hath known many fhips, denied to be laden with coals, only for cafting ballaft at Shields, to their extraordinary loffe, which is the caufe of coals being fold the dearer, they ftaying fo long for them.

(I) And that the faid mayor and burgeffes, being the fole caufe hereof, and likewife engroffe all provifions coming in by fea, and fets their own rates thereon, and takes exceffive *towl, one peck of every grain of corn. See ftat. 22. Hen. 8. 8.*. See chap. 44. (C), (A).

Tho. Cartwright, Mr. Symonds, and
Wil. Reavely, proves the like.

1. The pre-emption of tyn, foap, falt, cards, &c. was adjudged grievous, and why not coals, which is of as great ufe, nay more, as appears by ordinance of parliament, 1640; (A) alfo, they were damned by the judgement of the fage judges, in Sergeants-inn, upon a conference then had, before that parliament began, as being repugnant to the law.

2. And why a monopoly of coals, more upon the owners, then on any thing elfe in England? and more of them to be inflaved then any other people of England? I appeal to God, the whole world, as alfo to the coal-engroffers themfelves, whether it be juft? &c.

CHAP,

CHAP. XLV.

(A) DECEMBER, 1653, a charge was exhibited, to the committee for infpections, and advance of cuftomes, againft Mr. George Dawfon, collector of the cuftomes of Newcaftle, the contents being as follows, viz.

(B) That the ftate hath been, and is much wronged in their cuftomes in that port, by reafon fome of the faid cuftomers, are traders, merchants, &c. and many fhips vexatioufly troubled without juft caufe, onely by reafon they buy not their coals from them, and ordinarily give coals, for reparation, cuftome-free, as alfo, a fecond charge exhibited to the commiffioners of cuftomes, not doubting but to receive juftice at either place ; here follows the depofition, viz.

(c) Jonas Cudworth, of Newcaftle upon Tyne, draper, upon his oath,* in December laft, faid, that Mr. George Dawfon of Newcaftle, collector of the cuftomes, in the fame port, did exercife the trade of a free hoaft-man,* in the year 1651, and imployed for his fitter, one Tho. Read, who loaded feveral veffels with coals, and cleared them in the name of the faid Mr. Dawfon.

*Coal ingroffers.

(D) And in the year aforefaid, one John Grip, mafter of a hoy, belonging to Hamborough, was laden with coals, by the faid Thomas Read, and information being by this deponent, to the furveyor of the faid port, by name, Mr. Meriton, that the faid Grip had fhipped a great quantity of coals more, then he had cleared for, and paid the duty of cuftomes, the faid Mr. Meriton had acquainted the faid George Dawfon herewith, after which, notwithftanding information was made, and feizure alfo fhould have been made, he the faid George Dawfon did admit of a poft entry of a fmall quantity of the faid coals, and after cocket granted, and did not unload

unload the said vessel, to discover the fraud, and seize the same.

(E) This deponent further said, that about the same time, the said George Dawson did unload another vessel, belonging to Peter Hofman, of Dantzick, to his great damage, before any cocket granted, and refused to let any entry be made, though offered, before full loading, and for reparation thereof, he gave to the said master, four chalder of coals, custome free, and the said master, George Dawson, had, and hath parts of ships, * and trades over sea with coals. (See stat. 3. Hen. 7. 7.*) 14. Rich. 2. 10.

JONAS CUDWORTH.

(F) These are humbly to certifie, that David Lindiman, master of a ship, called the Fortune, of Statin, did load his ship with coals, in the said port of Newcastle upon Tyne, and cleared in the custome-house, for three score and twelve chalder of coals, and that Jonas Cudworth, of this town, came and told me, that the state was wronged of custome, for forty chaldron of coals, in that ship, and gave the names of the masters of keels, or boats, that laid the coals aboard, and requested they might be sworn, which was done, and the information found true. The said Mr. Lindiman did pay for forty chalder of coals, more then he had entered for in the custome-house, which custome amounted to fifty and odde pounds, all which, I humbly conceive, the state had been defrauded* of, if the said Jonas Cudworth had not informed thereof. See stat. 11. Hen. 6. 15.

THO. MERITON, surveyor.

Newcastle upon Tyne, 23. of March, 1643.

It is the old proverb, *foul birds bewrayes their own nest.*

If one ship could cheat the state, so much as fifty odd pounds custome, what do hundreds of ships do? See chap 46. (B.).

CHAP.

CHAP. XLVI.

(A) GEORGE PHILIPS, of London, matter, and captain of a ſhip, upon his oath, ſaid, that for his caſting ballaſt, at Shields, upon as ſufficient ballaſt-ſhoars as any can be, could not obtain his loading of coals, for doing thereof, being denied by the mayor, and burgeſſes of Newcaſtle, and lay five weeks for the ſame, and at laſt obtained favor from one Major Tolburſt, and Mr. Readnal, to furniſh him with keels or lighters, to fetch ſuch coals as he could procure, and when he had loaded his ſhip, Mr. George Dawſon, collector of the cuſtome-houſe, and * officer of the corporation of Newcaſtle, ſometimes mayor, alderman, juſtice of peace, and merchant, and Mr. George Blackſtone, cheque of the cuſtome-houſe, iſſued out a warrant, under the town-ſeal, and cuſtome-houſe-ſeal, to ſeize his ſhip and coals, upon the 19. of April, 1651, which warrant is extant amongſt the records at White-hall. See ſtat. 3. Hen. 7. 7.* 11. Hen. 6. 15.

GEORGE PHILIPS.

(B) Coales, the chalder, at Newcaſtle, doth coſt the maſters of ſhips, ten ſhillings the chalder, Newcaſtle meaſure, and one ſhilling cuſtome, ordained by queen Elizabeth.

For all coals, carried beyond ſea, by any Engliſhman, pays by the chalder, for coals and cuſtome, eleven ſhillings four pence, as by an act of parliament, of the 28. of March, 1651, appears.

For all coals, carried by any ſtranger, payes the chalder double, being for cuſtome per chalder, two and twenty ſhillings eight pence, and argiere duties, &c. in all ſix and twenty ſhillings and ten pence, cuſtome, beſides the price of coals and fraught.

For all coals at the market, in every port, two ſhillings per chalder, exciſe, towards building of frigots.

And

And for all coals, fold by the tun, one shilling per tun, and for all scotch coals, two shillings sixpence per tun.

(c) And yet, notwithstanding these impositions, coals might be sold for twenty shillings the chalder, all the year long, at London, with greater gain to the masters and seamen, if ballast shoars were at, or neer the Shields.

(d) Provisions for the relief of the multitude of shipping, above nine hundred sail, and the inhabitants there.

(e) Coals to be bought from the first hand, then there might be as many more voyages in the year, as now they make.

(f) The masters of ships, desires onely their due meafure, and then they would not regard the odd chalder given to the score, all which they are debarred of, most unjustly, for commonly where ships takes in at Newcastle, one hundred thirty six chalder of coals, and expects to make at London, two hundred and seventeen, or else lofeth, besides having bad coals a long voyage; there are computed three hundred and twenty coal keels, alias lighters, and every keel accounts to have carried every year, eight hundred chalder of coals to ships; then judge how many thousand London chalder is carried away. See chap. 23.

JOHN WRENHAM.
ROBERT REEX.

CHAP. XLVII.

People robbed in the open market, and others, onely passing through Newcastle. A. C. E. *Three Newcastle-men.* B. *Isabel Orde.* D. *John Williamson.*

(SEE PLATE 2. FIG. 2.)

(A) ELIZABETH LUMSDEL, upon her oath, faith, that one John Williamsons wife, and servants, having bought forty pounds worth of tobacco, (who dwelt at Braughton, in the county of Cumberland,) which said tobacco, all duties of excise, custome, or toul were paid, and carrying the same through Newcastle, towards Carlisle-market, one Mr. Huntley, and Mr. Stranguage, merchants, made * a seizure of the said tobacco and horses, by order from the magistrates, pretending it were foreign bought, and foreign sold, * and therefore confiscate to their use. The poor people petitioned sir Arthur Heislerigge for the same, who interceded hard with them for the restauration thereof, but it was refused, yet they, fearing sir Arthurs displeasure, sold the tobacco for thirty pound, and restored to the poor owner but fifteen pounds thereof.

(B) This deponent further affirms, upon her oath, that about the same time, one Isabel, wife to Henry Orde, sitting in open market, selling a role of tobacco, who had paid all duties, the said Mr. Huntley, and Mr. Stranguage, made * seizure, by strong hand, of the said tobacco from the poor woman, and would not acquaint them with the reason, whereupon, in passion, she called them robbing rascals, for which they sued her poor husband, in their own court, and put him to great expences; she, this deponent, with the said Isabel, hard petitioned judge Thorp for her tobacco, who sent for the two merchants, and demanded the reason of their taking away the poor woman womans tobacco in the open market, who produced a warrant from the mayor, who likewife was fent for, by name Mr. William Dawfon; the judge demanded of him, by what power he durft rob people in the market, who replyed, foreign bought, and foreign fold, my lord, but command was given by the faid judge to reftore the fame, but after departure it was not; then the judge granted a warrant for reftoring the fame upon his going away, and when it was fhewed the mayor, he fnatched it and put it up into his pocket, and would not reftore the faid tobacco, but fleighted the faid warrant. See ftat. * 3. Ed. 1. 24. 11. Ric. 2. 7. 27. Ed. 1. 5. 6. Ed. 6. 9. See chap. 49. 51.

ELIZ. LUMSDEL.

CHAP. XLVIII.

(A) LETTICE HUME, upon her oath, faid, that no victual or other provifions, coming in by fea, for the relief of Northumberland, or county of Durham, is permitted to be fold at Shields, but all is compelled to Newcaftle by the magiftrates, and there ingroffed after three market dayes, Tuefday, Saturday, and Tuefday, and payes double tole, * in and out, and pays double rates for the fame, and that fhe hath often known boats, and provifions, caft away, and peoples lives, in going and returning from Shields to Newcaftle, in ftormy weather, too and from the market; namely, one William Rea, with others, in the year 1650, at the fame time, and before, nor never any coroner fate upon any of the dead bodies, nor young Mr. Snape, &c. and that greater rates are given for provifions, being bought up by the townf-men, than might be had at the firft hand. See chap. 11.

(H), 44. (I), 49. (C), * ſtat. 3. Ed. 1. 20. 23. Ed. 3. 6. *

MARY HUME, LETTICE HUME, proves the like.

(B) Mr. Richard Blewet, brother to commiſſary Blewet, affirms, that in, or about the year 1649, rye was at ſixteen ſhillings the bowl, in Newcaſtle, none to be got for the poor, but from the merchant who had bought it all up, that the poor being in great want, ſir Arthur Haſlerigge cauſed the ſaid commiſſary, to lay out a thouſand pounds of the publick ſtock upon rye, from the firſt ſhips that came, and to ſell it for the relief of the poor, four ſhillings under the market, which was done.

(B) The merchants of Newcaſtle, proffered to his ſaid brother, the market price for all the corn he had bought, which was ſixteen ſhillings the bowl, when they ſaw the ſaid commiſſary ſell, for eleven ſhillings per bowl to the poor, and the commiſſary was a great gainer at eleven ſhillings, and paid as much as the merchant.

(C) And by reaſon the ſaid commiſſary did refuſe, ſome of them threatened, if ten thouſand pounds would break his back in ſuit, for daring to ſell corn in their town, he not being a free-man, it ſhould. This information I had from Mr. Blewet, who will make it good upon his oath, when called, and from Mr. Nich. Ogle. They will neither doe good, nor ſuffer good to be done, much like the dog in a manger. See ſtat. 5. 6. Edw. 6. 14. 23. Edw. 3. 6. 2. Edw. 6. 15. 5. Eliz. 12.

CHAP. XLIX.

(A) WILLIAM REAVELY, of Lyn, maſter of a ſhip, upon his oath, ſaid, that by reaſon of the ſhips not caſting ballaſt at Shields, above four, if not five voyages, are loſt in the year compleat.

(B) That all provisions brought in by sea, are compelled up to Newcastle, and there ingrossed into the free-mens hands; people often going to market have lost their lives, and many starved to death in the two counties, which cannot get to Newcastle market, in the winter season, by reason of the great storms of snows, and the river frozen, and no market allowed for the counties relief at Shields, where many thousand of passengers, sea-men, and inhabitants are, being twelve miles from any market in the same county.

(c) That he, this deponent, and ships company, hath often been constrained to go to sea, without bread or beer, none being to be got at Shields on a sudden, and have drunk water for above five daies, which hath so weakened his men, that they were in great danger of their lives, and that from Newcastle, they often send down dead beer, and the casks, but half, or three parts full, from the brewers of the said town, and bread wanting above two pence weight in the shilling, and not looked after by the magistrates.

(D) That they the said mayor, and burgesses of Newcastle, aforesaid, did ruin one Mr. Johnson, and Mr. Hilton, for brewing at Shields, for the relief of the ships, and that they rooked from him, this deponent, twelve barrels of beer, which he brought from Lyn, for the relief of the poor at Shields, and made it confiscate, arrested him, and cast him into prison, sued him, and made him enter into sixty pound bond, never to bring in any more, also kept a bag of hops, which was sent to a friend in Northumberland, and that he hath known them often do the like to others, they being judges, jurors, and witnesses in their own cause.

(E) That they take excessive tole,* above a peck of corn of every grain brought to be sold by vessels, besides all other duties.

(F) That the said magistrates force men to swear against themselves, *and will not tollerate any gentleman, to build ballast-shoars upon their own land.

(G) And that he, this deponent, hath feen ballaft warrants, figned by one of the magiftrates,* only for keels to carry up ballaft from Shields, and hath feen the keel-men caft it into the river, in the fouth road, to the rivers great damage,* and often dirt caft into the river, by fervants, brought out of the gates, when no watchmen were kept. See chap. 39. (A), 12. 4. 14. (C), 47. (B), 51. See ftat. 27. Ed. 1. * 51. Hen. 3. 15.* 11. Hen. 7. 4. * 5. 6. Ed. 6. 9.* 3. Ed. 1. 20.* 17. k. Char.*

WILLIAM REAVELY.

(G) Hugh Farrow, of Lyn, mafter of a fhip, upon his oath, faid, that he and his fhips company having lyen fo long at Shields, for a fair wind, with the fleet, that when they had fpent all their provifions, at no time could obtain any from Shields, by reafon obftructed by the magiftrates, and having fent up his boat and fome of his men for fome at Newcaftle, the wind came fair, and on a fudden the fhips all fet fail to fea, fo that he, this deponent muft loofe the protection of the fleet, and hazard himfelf to the mercy of the enemy, or muft leave his men and boat behind, which the latter he did, and was conftrained to drink ftinking water for four daies, for want of beer, which might be conveniently got at Shields, and he was in greater danger of lofing his fhip, for want of his men.

HEN. FARROW.

CHAP. L.

(A) TO. Gardner, of London, upon her oath, faid, that within this feven and twenty years, or hereabouts, fhe knew the ufual practice of the mayor, and burgeffes of Newcaftle, was to ingrofs all

all provifions into their hands, as corn, &c. and have kept it* in their corn lofts ‖ till fo dear, and at fuch high and exceffive rates, that moft people could not buy it, and that the people of Northumberland, and county of Durham, being in great want for bread, that many were conftrained to let their beafts blood, and made cakes thereof, to eat inftead of bread, and in the fpring time many of thofe beafts dyed, being over-blooded.

(B) Other poor people killed their coal-horfes for food, fome eating dogs, and cats, and ftarved, many ftarved to death*, fixteen, or feventeen dead, in a hole together; and yet at the fame time many hundred bowles of corn caft into the river, being* rotten, and mouldy, and eaten with rats, and fome of thofe people boafting, they hoped to fee the day a bowle of corns price fhould buy a filk gown. This was not in the time of war, and the countries might have had plenty, if it had not been ingroffed by them. See ftat. 5. Eliz. 12.* 23. Ed. 3. 6.*.

Jo. GARDNER.

Major WILL. BURTON, late member of parliament, THO. HESILWOOD, and WIL. REAVELY, proves the like.

(B) Richard Tayler, upon his oath, faid, that the mayor, and burgeffes of Newcaftle, do compel all iron and other neceffaries, which comes in by fea, for the falt-pans and collieries ufe, at and near Shields, to be carried up to Newcaftle, and unladen upon their town-key, at the charge of the owner, and to pay toule, and the fame veffels forced to fail back to Shields empty, and often fuch veffels finks by the way, and their own veffels muft be hired, at their own rates, to carry it back again to Shields, being fometimes fourteen daies in getting down thither, though prefent ufe be for the fame, and

divers

divers times cast away, so that ships utterly refuse to bring such commodities, to be put to such unnecessary and needless trouble and charge, and this is done constantly, notwithstanding all duties are paid, and the ship or vessel comes onely for salt at Shields, where it is made, and not to Newcastle, where they have no business. See stat. 21. Hen. 8. 18.

RICH. TATLER.
WILL. REAVELY.

(c) It were less damage to the commonwealth, for allowing seamen, for their encouragements, 5l. custom-free of goods, then thus to be abused by meer pretences of loss of custom, especially, by such who wrongs the customs. See chap. 45. (F).

CHAP. LI.

(A) ALEXANDER SYMONDS, of Lin, merchant, upon his oath, said, that all commodities, as well dead victual, as other merchandize, are compelled up to Newcastle, which comes in by sea, and there, by the mayor and burgesses, are ingrossed and bought up by them; nothing to be landed elsewhere but at Newcastle, notwithstanding all ships do lye at Shields, and passengers; and often in stormy weather, and river frozen, none can pass too and fro, for any relief from thence, and none to be had elsewhere, and if there be any, it is seized on by them of Newcastle, and confiscate to their own use, namely, beer from one Will. Reavely, and divers others. See chap. 11. (N), 47. (A), 49. (D), 50. (A).

ALEXANDER SYMONDS, and THOMAS CARTWRIGHT, depose the like.

(B) Captain

(B) Captain James Greenaway, of London, affirms, that his ship was at Shields, in company with a fleet of loaden ships, where they all had lyen a long time, for a fair wind, and had often spent their provisions; on a sudden the wind came fair, and the whole fleet set sail for London; he, this deponent, having spent all his bread, could get but two dozen at both Shields, yet was necessitated to set to sea with the fleet, otherwise had lost their protection, if staid till he sent to Newcastle, for bread.

(B) The whole fleet being at sea, the wind came cross, being a violent storm, that it was five daies before they could get so high as Scarborough, some twenty leagues from Newcastle, and then the storm ceased, and he, this deponent, got ashoar to Scarborough, for bread, when, the wind coming fair, the fleet sailed out of sight, so he lost their protection and company; (G) he, getting aboard, and sailing after them, was taken by a Dunkirk man of war, lost his ship, goods, and money, his ship being worth 800l. goods, 200l. and money, 400l. all which might have been saved, if bread, beer, and provisions had been admitted to be sold at Shields. Onely are hindered by the tyrannical power of the mayor, and burgesses of Newcastle.

JAMES GREENAWAY.

(H) John Houlden, upon his oath, said, that in or about the year 1648, a master of a ship was arrested, and imprisoned, onely for selling of a little corn, to commissary West, by the mayor of Newcastle, he alleadging the town was not served, but sir Arthur Hazlerigge caused the mayor to release the said master, and demanded by what power, law, or right, they ought to imprison any man, for selling his own commodity in the market or key, and told Mr. Ledger, then mayor, if he did not release him, the souldiers should.

JOHN HOLDEN.

CHAP.

CHAP. LIII.

Many poor women imprisoned, and hanged for witches.

A. *Hangman.* B. *Bellman.* C. *Two sergeants.* D. *Witch-finder taking his money for his work.*

(SEE PLATE 3. FIG. 1.)

(A) JOH. WHEELER, of London, upon his oath, said, that in, or about the years 1649, and 1650, being at Newcaftle, heard that the magiftrates had fent two of their fergeants, namely, Thomas Shevel, and Cuthbert Nicholfon, into Scotland, to agree with a fcotch-man, who pretended knowledge to finde out witches, by pricking them with pins, to come to Newcaftle, where he fhould try fuch who fhould be brought to him, and to have twenty-fhillings a peece, for all he could condemn as witches, and free paffage thither and back again.

(B) When the fergeants had brought the faid witch-finder on horfe-back, to town, the magiftrates fent their bell-man through the town, ringing his bell, and crying, all people that would bring in any complaint againft any woman for a witch, they fhould be fent for, and tryed by the perfon appointed.

(C) Thirty women were brought into the town-hall, and ftript, and then openly had pins thruft into their bodies, and moft of them was found guilty, * near twenty feven of them by him, and let afide.

(D) The faid reputed witch-finder, acquainted lieut. colonel Hobfon, that he knew women, whether they were witches or no, by their looks, and when the faid perfon was fearching of a perfonable, and good-like woman, the faid colonel replyed, and faid,
surely

Plate III Fig 1 page 114

Fig II see page 117

Published Oct'r 1st 1796 by D. Akenhead & Sons, Newcastle upon Tyne

surely this woman is none, and need not be tryed, but the scotch-man said she was, for the town said she was, and therefore he would try her; and presently in sight of all the people, laid her body naked to the waste, with her cloaths over her head, by which fright and shame, all her blood contracted into one part of her body, and then he ran a pin into her thigh, and then suddenly let her coats fall, and then demanded whether she had nothing of his in her body, but did not bleed, but she being amazed, replied little, then he put his hand up her coats, and pulled out the pin, and set her aside as a guilty person, and child of the devil, and fell to try others whom he made guilty.

(E) Lieutenant colonel Hobson, perceiving the alteration of the foresaid woman, by her blood settling in her right parts, caused that woman to be brought again, and her cloaths pulled up to her thigh, and required the scot to run the pin into the same place, and then it gushed out of blood, and the said scot cleared her, and said, she was not a child of the devil.

(F) So soon as he had done, and received his wages, he went into Northumberland, to try women there, where he got of some, three pound a peece, but Henry Ogle, esq. a late member of parliament, laid hold on him, and required bond of him, to answer the sessions, but he got away for Scotland, and it was conceived, if he had staid, he would have made most of the women in the north, witches, for mony.

(G) The names of the prisoners that were to be executed, being kept in prison till the assizes, and then condemned by the jury, being burgesses, were, Matthew Bulmer, Eliz. Anderson, Jane Hunter, Mary Pots, Alice Hume, Elianor Rogerson, Margaret Muffet, Margaret Maddison, Eliz. Brown, Margaret Brown, Jane Copeland, Ann Watson, Elianor Henderson, Elizabeth Dobson, and Katherine

rine Coultor. These poor souls never confessed any thing, but pleaded innocence, and one of them, by name, Margaret Brown, beseeched God that some remarkable sign might be seen, at the time of their execution, to evidence their innocency, and as soon as ever she was turned off the ladder, her blood gushed out upon the people, to admiration of the beholders.

    JOHN WHEELER, ELIANOR LUMSDEL, and
     BARTHOLOMEW HODSHON, proves the
    like.

(H) The said witch-finder was laid hold on in Scotland, cast into prison, indicted, arraigned, and condemned for such like villanie, exercised in Scotland; and upon the gallows, he confessed he had been the death of above two hundred and twenty women, in England, and Scotland, for the gain of twenty shillings a peece, and beseeched forgiveness, and was executed.

(I) The judgement, nor execution, is not in question, nor questioned, being ordinary, but onely, it being desired to know, by what law the magistrates of Newcastle could send into another nation, for a mercinary person, to try women for witches, and a bell-man, to cry for them to be brought in, and twenty shillings a peece given him, to condemn them?

(K) Query, and by what law men are hired to give evidence, to take away peoples lives, and the convicted estates to come to the jurors, being extraordinary.

The lord protector, commands all judges, justices, and witnesses, to appear to execute justice, and give evidence gratis.

Queen Elizabeth, by her charter, grants to the mayor and burgesses, all fines, and felons goods in that town and liberties. Zech. 11. 5. See chap. 58. (C.D).

            CHAP.

CHAP. LV.

A. *Robert Sharp.*   B. *Ann Bidleſtone.*

(SEE PLATE 3. FIG. 2.)

(A) JOHN WILLIS, of Ipſwich, upon his oath, ſaid, that he, this deponent, was in Newcaſtle, ſix months ago, and there he ſaw one Ann Bidleſtone, drove through the ſtreets, by an officer of the ſame corporation; holding a rope in his hand, the other end faſtened to an engine, called the branks, which is like a crown, it being of iron, which was muſled,* over the head and face, with a great gap, or tongue of iron, forced into her mouth, which forced the blood out, and that is the puniſhment which the magiſtrates do inflict upon chiding, and ſcoulding women, and that he hath often ſeen the like done to others.

(B) He, this deponent, further affirms, that he hath ſeen men drove up and down the ſtreets, with a great tub, or barrel, opened in the ſides, with a hole in one end, to put through their heads, and ſo cover their ſhoulders and bodies, down to the ſmall of their legs, and then cloſe the ſame, called the new faſhioned cloak, and ſo make them march to the view of all beholders; and this is their puniſhment for drunkards, or the like.

(C) This deponent further teſtifies, that the merchants, and ſhoe-makers of the ſaid corporation, will not take any apprentice under ten years ſervitude, and knoweth many bound for the ſame terme, and cannot obtain freedome without. 5 Eliz. 4.

Theſe are ſuch practices as are not granted by their charter law, and are repugnant to the known laws of England.

(D) Drunkards are to pay a fine of five ſhillings to the poor, to be paid within one week, or be ſet

in

in the flocks fix hours; for the fecond offence, to be bound to the good behaviour. 1. k. James, 9. 21. 7.

(E) Scoulds are to be duckt over head and ears, into the water, in a ducking-ftool.

(F) And apprentices are to ferve but feven years, 5. Eliz. 4.

I was certainly informed, by perfons of worth, that the punifhments above, are but gentle admonitions, to what they knew was acted by two magiftrates of Newcaftle, one for killing a poor workman of his own, and being queftioned for it, and condemned, compounded with king James for it, paying to a fcotch lord his weight in gold and filver, every feven years, or thereabouts, &c. the other magiftrate found a poor man cutting a few horfe-fticks in his wood, for which offence, he bound him to a tree, and whipt him to death. Related by William Wall, vintner, in Gates-fide, Tho. Watfon, fcrivenor, on fand-hill, and Ralph Watfon, late minifter in Northumberland.

CHAP. LVI.

(A) FIVE and twenty years ago, upon the trial with the mayor, and burgeffes of Newcaftle, and fir Robert * Heath, the judgement of the moft ancient and experienced mafters of the trinity-houfe, in London, were required, in anfwer to the town of Newcaftles objections, as is upon record in the trinity-houfe.

(B) Newcaftles faith, if ballaft-fhoars be fuffered to be built at, or near the Shields* it would hinder the towns trade, and endanger the river of Tyne; neither can any ballaft-fhoars be built at Shields, below a full fea-mark, or in any part of the river,
by

by any but Newcaſtle, by reaſon all that ground, to a full ſea mark, on both ſides of the river, is the towns, by charter, from Sparhawke to Headwin ſtreams, fourteen miles in length. See chap. 20. (A), 19. (E.G).

(c) Anſwer, to the firſt. It will not hinder the town of trade, but advantage the whole nation, eſpecially that town, by reaſon double trade will be drove thereby, and cauſe coals to be cheaper at half rates, then now they are at, and the river better preſerved.

(D) Secondly, it will better the river; for inning of void and waſte grounds, and flats in rivers, cauſeth the ſtreams to be more ſtrong, and run more ſwift, which thereby will ſcowr and cleanſe the channel, and conſequently gain more water to the river, preſerve the banks from falling into it, help navigation; for the deeper the water, the more navigable, the leſſe danger, and more ſafety for ſhips. See chap. 19, (H)*.

(E) It is alſo anſwered, by others, if the ground, to a full ſea-mark, be theirs, then why ſhould they proffer to king Charles,* two hundred pound, for Jarrow-ſlike, 1637, all which the water covers, and is within a full ſea-mark. See 20. chap. (C.D).

(F) Alſo, why ſhould Thomas Bonner, the alderman, buy ſir Henry Gibs his ballaſt ſhoar, to a low water-mark, at Jarrow, for his uſe, from the town, (were it theirs before?)

(G) And why ſhould Mr. Gibſon * ſwear, none of that ground, which they claim to a full ſea-mark is theirs? See 34. chap. (B).

(H) In the treaſury, at Weſtminſter, thoſe ancient records, will quickly decide the controverſie, making it appear, that the one third part of the river, on the ſouth-ſide, belongs to the gentry of the county of Durham, and all grounds to a low water-mark; and the like on the north-ſide, to the gentry of Northumberland; and the other third part free, for ſhips and

veſſels

veſſels to ſail too and fro, for the relief of the inhabitants. See chap. 34. (A), (*), (B). See chap. 4. (*).

(1) It is too much, that the corporation ſhould be lords of both the ſea and all the land, and it is too little, the commoners, in both counties, ſhould have neither ſea nor land, being born to all alike.

A quo warranto would know, by what power they claim one ſhilling for every ballaſt bill, one ſhilling for every ſalt bill, three pence for every chalder of coals, two pence for every weigh of ſalt, and eight pence the tun, for all ballaſt, and I am confidently perſwaded (K) would void them all, for they are neither cuſtomary, nor warrantable by law, (ſo unlawful;) as for other duties, as tunage and poundage, cuſtomes, lightage, otherwiſe called beaconage, boyage, for maintaining of peers, and ancoridge with tole, it will hardly be queſtioned, except abuſed. Let them complain that are agrieved, &c. See ſtat. 30. Edw. 1. 1301.

Inſtead of a mayor, in that, and ſuch like corporations, a king Cattelus ſpirit to govern, were better, who hanged up all oppreſſors of the poor, for an example, whereby he reigned twenty yeers in peace; alſo a Lud, who made good laws, and took away all uſages that were bad, and reigned long in peace and plenty.

CHAP.

CROMWELL.

HIS EXCELLENCIE, OLIVER CROMWELL,

Generall of all the forces of England, Scotland, and Ireland, chancellour of the univerſity of Oxford, lord protector of England, Scotland, and Ireland.

CHAP. LIV.

An act for a free-trade, in the river of Tyne, for coals, ſalt, &c.

(A) WHEREAS trade and commerce is become now, more than formerly, the intereſt of this nation, and it is therefore the duty, as well as the wiſdome of this parliament, to ſecure and advance the fame, and in order thereunto, and for other great ends of honour and ſafety, to increaſe the ſhipping, and incourage navigation; and whereas a great part of the ſtock, and wealth of this nation, lyes in the well huſbanding and managing of thoſe home commodities, of coals and ſalt, milſtones, glaſſe, the chief trade whereof is exerciſed upon the river of Tyne, and in the county of Northumberland and Durham.

(B) And whereas the parliament hath been informed of great exorbitances, done, and committed, by the town and corporation of Newcaſtle, upon pretence and colour of powers, priviledges, and franchiſes, granted to the ſaid corporation, whereby it appears, (c) that the free and quick trade of thoſe ſtaple commodities, hath been much obſtructed, the river made dangerous, and in many places almoſt un-navigable, and encreaſe of ſhipping, ſo conſiderable a nurcery of marriners, greatly ruined, and navigation too much diſcouraged; for remedy herein,

(D) Be it enacted, declared, and ordained, by this preſent parliament, and by the authority thereof, that all former powers, priviledges, and grants, made,

made, and granted to the town and corporation of Newcaftle, or to any other perfon, or perfons whatfoever, for the confervancy of the river of Tyne, be, and are hereby repealed, made void, and null, and the committee of the admiralty, by authority of parliament, or any five of them, be, and are hereby authorized, and required, to nominate and appoint, fit and able perfons, as well of the counties of Northumberland and Durham, fea-coaft, and port of London, as of the town and corporation of Newcaftle, to have the charge of, and to be confervators of the river of Tyne, and to inveft, and impower the faid perfons, with all priviledges and power neceffary, to enable them for the better, and more effectual carrying on, and performance of the faid fervice.

(E) And the faid commiffioners are hereby further impowered, and enable from time to time, to give, and prefcribe unto the faid confervators, rules, and inftructions, for to obferve and purfue, and to require obedience thereunto, and to receive and examine complaints, and to hear witneffes, upon oath, (which oath, they, the commiffioners, or any three of them, are hereby enabled to adminifter) and to punifh offenders, by reafonable fine, and punifhment, by imprifonment, and to difplace, and to remove confervators, upon juft and reafonable caufe, and to leffen, or adde to their number, as they fhall fee caufe, and to direct and order all other matters requifite, and neceffary, for the confervancy of fo famous and commodious a river, and for preventing of all fuch damages, mifchiefs, and newfances, as may hurt, or ruine the fame, and to fettle a ftipend upon the faid confervators, and to direct the fame, and other neceffaries, and incident charges, to be allowed, and iffue out of the profits of the faid river.

(F) And be it further enacted, and ordained, that fufficient and well fenced ballaft fhoars, keys, and
ſteaths,

fteaths, be built and erected, either at Shieids, or fuch other convenient place, as the faid confervators, or the major part of them fhall think fitting; and the faid confervators, are authorifed and required, to ufe and direct, all good wayes and means, according to fuch powers and directions, as they fhall from time to time receive, from the faid commiffioners of the admiralty, to prevent and remedy all damages, that may happen, by loffe of fhips, and mens lives, at fea, by cafting their ballaft over-board, or into the river, at unfeafonable times, or unfitting places, or from the ballaft-fhoars, being carelefsly kept, through great winds, rains, or other cafualties, wafhing down the ballaft, and that from henceforth, no mafters of any fhips, or other veffels, be conftrained to go up the river, and to heave out their ballaft, at the fhoars belonging to the town of Newcaftle, or be hindred to load coals, or difcharge their ballaft, where they may, with moft conveniency and fafety, perform it, as well to the road-fteads itfelf, as to their fhipping.

(G) And further, that all mafters of fhips, trading to the faid river of Tyne, have hereby liberty and power, to make ufe within the faid river, of what fhip-carpenter, or fhip-wright, or other artificers, or perfons, they pleafe, and find fitteft for their own conveniency, in times of diftreffe and neceffity.

(H) And of what able fea-men they fhall think fit, for pilots.

(I) And have hereby liberty to buy, or take in, at any place of the faid port, or river, bread, and beer, and other neceffaries, for their own fpending and victualling.

(K) And that all goods and provifions, which come in by fea, for the ufe of the falt works, colleries, and other buildings, at, or near the Shields, may be delivered at the Shields, courfe being taken for paying and fatisfying all duties, payable for the faid goods and provifions.

(L.) And

(L) And all perſons, who are willing, are hereby encouraged, and have liberty, to build ſhips and veſſels, on the ſaid river, for the encreaſe of trade and navigation.

(M) And that all this be done without any fine, impriſonment, confiſcation, or other moleſtation of any perſon, veſſell, or goods, for, or in reference to any of the premiſes, any law, uſage, practice, cuſtome, priviledge, grant, charter, or other pretence whatſoever, to the contrary, notwithſtanding: Provided alwayes,

(N) And it is hereby enacted, that no ſhip, or veſſell whatſoever, that ſhall bring in any kind of merchandize, or grain, for the proper uſe of the town of Newcaſtle, uſually coming to the ſaid town of Newcaſtle, and places adjacent, beyond, ſhall deliver, or land the ſame, or any part thereof, at any other place, within the ſaid harbour or port, but at the ſaid town, or, as near to it as formerly have been accuſtomed.

(O) And to the end ſo uſeful a commodity, as that of ſea-coal, wherein the poor of this commonwealth are ſo principally concerned, may come cheaper to the market, and that coal-owners may not be in a worſe condition, then the reſt of the free people of this nation, Be it enacted, and ordained, that the ſaid coal-owners, in the reſpective counties, adjacent to that river, may, and have hereby liberty, to let leaſes of their coal-pits, and to ſell their coals to whom they pleaſe, as well to ſhips, as elſe-where, for benefit of the public, though they be not free of that corporation of Newcaſtle, due courſe being taken for ſecuring, paying, and ſatisfying to the ſtate, all duties payable thereupon.

And be it further enacted, that North-Shields, in the county of Northumberland, be made a market-town, two dayes in the week, to be holden, on Munday, and Thurſday, for the relief of the country, the garriſon of Tynemouth caſtle, the great confluence

fluence of people, and fleets of ships, and that the
commiffioners of the great feal, be hereby authorized,
to iffue out fuch powers as are requifite, and ufually
done, to other markets in the commonwealth.

*This is the copy of what was to have paffed, after
debate, if the late parliament had continued, &c.
appointed to be drawn up by order.*

HAVING given a fhort relation of the fad events
by charters, and acted by fubjects, I fhall
now trouble your eye and ear, to hear what kings
have done to thefe poor northern people formerly,
therefore now deliverance is expected, &c. leaving it
to the judgement of the reader, to judge whether
it be not time, &c. viz.

The danes laid claim to the crown of England,
the kings laid claim to the peoples lives, and corporations to their eftates, (what was free?) judge what
reafon England hath to fubmit to thofe illegal charter-
laws, invented by a prerogative, whofe ufurpation was
not to be owned, as by the fequell appears. King Harrold who affumed the crown of England to himfelf,
lead an army to battell in Suffex, where William the
conqueror, baftard earle of Normandy, met him, having the affiftance of the earle of Flanders, by reafon
he was promifed a good part of England, if he con-
quered it, at which place, king Harrold was killed,
and fixty feven thoufand, nine hundred feventy four
englifh-men, in the year 1060, at which time he con-
fumed many towns, fubduing where ever he came,
except Kent, who contracted, to hold their land in
gavel-kind, all England elfe being over-come by
this faid ftranger, &c.

When the Normans ruled England, the laws were
in that tongue, but they being extinguifhed, we find
the benefit of our laws, in our own tongue, and
doubts not but to be reftored to our ancient right,
for fo long as monarchs were rulers, monopolies
were

were in force, but now such power being thrown out of doors, and being become a civill free state, under the government of our own free-born, chosen, according to the command of God, as Deut. 17. 14. 15. by which monopolizers dare not assume to petition for a revival of such their illegal grants, being found to be the greatest of evills in a commonwealth.

All kings were sworn, that justice should neither be bought nor sold, nor any hindred from it, to ordain good laws, and withstand all rapines, and false judgements.

Charters are no other than commissions, impowring persons, uncapable of the laws, to be judges and justices, in every respective corporation, which charter and commission is sold, and the members thereof are judges, in their own causes. So justice is both bought, and sold, besides breach of oath, neither can a foreigner obtain any right, if it be against the said corporation, so that it is right in these judges judgement to do wrong.

I shall give you a short relation of the miseries, the county of Northumberland hath tasted of, to this day, from William the conqueror, and what little need there is Newcastle should so tyrannize over them, &c.

WILLIAM the conqueror, having killed many, and destroyed the land, and brought under his subjection, the people, caused such who did oppose his forces, at Ely, to have their legs and hands cut off, and their eyes put out, and then gave liberally to all his Norman race, earldoms, baronies, bishopricks, honours, mannors, dignities, and farms, all being got by the sword; upon his divisions, &c. the earle of Flanders sent to know what part he should have for assisting him, who sent him word, nothing at all, by reason all was but little enough for himself; then he gave to his son, Robert Cuming, the earldom of Northumberland, who in possessing of of it, acted such cruelty, with his army, which came againſt Malcolm, king of the ſcots. The ſaid Robert built the caſtle, called the Newcaſtle, upon the river of Tyne, in the county of Northumberland, about which was built the town, called Newcaſtle, the town taking its name from the Newcaſtle, and not the caſtle from the town; the ſaid Northumberland being ſo oppreſſed, that they fell upon Robert, ſon to the conqueror, killed him, and his whole army, upon which, William the conqueror ſent another army, who had command, to kill both men, women, and children, who did it, and waſted the whole county, that for nine yeers there was not any food to be got, and ſuch who had hid themſelves in coal-pits, and other places, were conſtrained to eat dogs and cats, dead horſes, and mens fleſh, and many of them ſtarved to death, all which nine years time, not any ground tilled.

Northumberland being recruted, and moſt ſhamefully abuſed, by the biſhop of Durham, who killed Leviſus, was killed by them, for which, William the conqueror ſent down Odo, with an army, who totally laid Northumberland to waſte, cut off the heads of all the people, after they had diſmembered them.

Little of confeſſion, or repentance, was by king John, as was by William the conqueror, for he, upon his arreſt, at the ſuit of death, confeſſed he had committed many outrages, and won England by the ſword, and not by inheritance, and was heartily ſorry for the wrongs he had done, and required his body to be buried, at Cain, in Normandy. When he was dead, they would not afford him a burial-place, till ſuch time as one of his relations was conſtrained, to purchaſe ſo much ground, but ſoon after they defaced his tomb, took up his bones, and brake them, and caſt them away.

In the fifteenth year of king Richard the ſecond, the ſcots burnt all the towns of Northumberland, and

and the north, as far as York, except Rippon, who redeemed themselves with a sum of mony.

In the sixth year of king Edward the third, 1332, a great battel was fought between the englifh and the fcots, near Barwick, where was killed, eight earls, fifteen hundred horfe, and thirty five thousand foot.

In the thirteenth year of king Edward the third, 1339, an inundation of water furmounted the wall of Newcaftle, and broke down fix pearches in length, and drowned one hundred and fixty perfons, neer the wark knowl.

In the year 1345, William Douglas lead into Northumberland, above thirty thoufand fcots, and fired many towns, but was overcome, by a ftratagem with bifhop Ogle.

The next year, 1346, king David, king of the fcots, entered Northumberland, with a great army, and fought at Nevils-Croffe, where he was overthrown, himfelf taken prifoner, by one Copland of Northumberland, who had five hundred pound per annum, given to him, and to his heirs for ever.

In king Richard the feconds dayes, 1379, the fcots entered England, and killed all men, women, and children, in the north parts, notwithftanding the plague was forely amongft them.

1383. The fcots entered England, and lead all the people away prifoners, that were in Northumberland, and laid that county to wafte.

1384. They entered again, and did the like.

1389. The fcots again invaded England, where a great battel was fought, at Otterborn, in Northumberland, where they were over-thrown, and eleven hundred killed, and thirty thoufand put to flight, who, upon their flight, killed men, women, and fucking babes, and filled houfes with people, two hundred in a houfe, and then fhut the doors, and fired the houfes.

1399.

1399. King Richard the fecond, caufed feventeen counties to be indicted, pretending they were all againſt him, with the duke of Glocefter, Arundel, and Warwick, and commanded them all, to give it under their hands, and feals, that they were traytors, though indeed they never were, and then he makes them pay, fome a thoufand pound, fome more, fome leſſe.

King Henry the fourth. Great fights were between Douglas and Piercy, in the north.

And in the years 1639, and 1643, and 1648, it being well known to all, the mifery they brought upon the north, and heavy impofitions, both upon the north, and fouth parts, as appears, in the clofe of the epiftle to the reader, &c.

It is no fmall mercy, that we now live fo in peace, here being none of thofe bloody times; and our anceftors would willingly have enjoyed this mercy; and we hunger after blood, which they wallowed in. What bloody minded men are thefe? I wifh them in better minds, and to be contented with that, which, in former times, could not be obtained.

Many have admired the poverty of Northumberland, as well they may, for what with the bloody tyrants, the fcots, on the north of that poor county, and oppreſſive corporation of Newcaftle, on the fouth thereof, bounded in with the high-lands, on the weft, and the fea, on the eaft, that it can get nothing but ftrokes, and worried out of what they have, and not being tollerated to make ufe of their own, and cold blafts from the fea; but it would be otherwife, if fuch gentlemen might be re-imburfed, for fuch fums of money, as they would expend, to vend coals out of Hartly, Blithe, and Bedlington rivers, which be convenient places, to vend them at, after fome charge, which would be done, by having, either their money again, or cuftome free, for fome years, to re-imburfe them, which would not onely make that poor county as rich as any is, but reduce the excessive rates of coals, and salt, and bring in many thousands per annum, into the public revenew, &c. enable the people to be serviceable, and abundantly increase trade, and navigation, as also, there being as good coals, as possibly can be burnt, which now lyes, &c. and others, not knowing their right, is stript of it.

But if one thing they look after, which is to examine some records, they may perceive what is their rights, and which was, especially in a book, lodged in the exchequer, made in the year 1080, it being called *Domus Dei*, or *Dooms day*, being a perfect survey, of all the lands in England, the rent, value, quantity, &c. by which, William the conqueror, taxed the whole nation, and it goeth by the name of the role of Winton, being ordered to be kept in Winchester, and recites the earldomes, hundreds, tythings, woods, parks, and farms, in every territory and precinct, with plowlands, meadows, marshes, acres, &c. what tenements, and tenants; then the corporation of Newcastle, might be as glad, to keep what is their own, as they are to take from others, &c.

CHAP. LVII.

THE reason of my collecting these few statutes is, to shew how they are intrenched upon, by an illegal charter, and pressing upon a remedy, shall cite Poulton, which is, that seeing we have all received, and allow it for truth, that the ignorance of the law, doth excuse none of offence, and also, that the law doth help the watchful, and not the sloathful man.

Therefore

Therefore, it behoveth each perfon, firft, to feek the knowledge of thofe laws, under which he doth live, and whereby he is to receive benefit, or to fuftain peril, and next, with all induftry, to frame his obedience unto them, or humbly to fubmit himfelf, to the cenfure of them.

And though we find by experience, that fome men, by the fluggifhneffe of their natures, others, by the carelefneffe of their own welfares, and a third fort, wholly given over to pleafures and vanities, do little refpect to know, and leffe to obey, our criminal, and capital laws, being things of great moment, and importance, and therefore do oftentimes tafte the fmart of them, and repent of their follies, when it is too late.

Many there be, that by reading, defires to conceive them, others, for increafe of their knowledge, others, in their actions, to be directed by them, therefore to content fuch, as knoweth not, as yet, thefe heads, that they may know what they condemn, and do tend to the breach of the peace of the realm, and to the diflike of all the good members thereof, and what punifhments fhe hath impofed, upon the tranfgreffors therein, and by whom, and in what manner to be inflicted, efpecially, upon murder, robbery, riots, forgery, perjury, extortion, and oppreffion, in any of which cafes, any perfon maketh it his own caufe, and doth, in a fort, take it to be done to himfelf, and ought to reduce the tranfgreffor, nay, his highneffe, by his oath, and all people elfe, are bound to punifh them, as being tranfgreffors of his laws, and difquieters of the peace, therefore ought to be rooted out, as the hufbandman the thiftle, from the good corn, and the gardner his nettles, from his fweet flowers, wherefore, feeing a guilty perfon, in any of the offences aforefaid, is perfecuted in deed, or confent, by all, wifhing well to the weal-publick, or their own private eftate.

It

It is requisite, that good men, which eschew to offend, for the love of virtue, and evill men, which fear to offend, for the dread of punishment, should both know those laws, which they are to make use of, and the penalties, which be threatened to the infringers thereof, to the intent, the good man having a will to stand, may trust to his feet, remain firm, and continue his integrity, and the evill man, beginning to stagger, may bend his endeavour to stay, and slide no further, (this labour) being to the intent, that the well meaning-man, being made the better, and he, or they, that before were lewdly disposed, the lesse hurtful, may all, at the last, meet and joyn in seeking, and furtherance of that peace, which will be comfortable to the lord protector, and nation, and pleasing, both to God and man.

These laws are preservers of the peace, and layes heavy punishments, upon the withstanders, or deniers thereof, they are his highnesse privy councellors, incessantly, respecting the preservation of his person and dignity, they be as his gentlemen pensioners, attending daily his presence, to do him all honor and service, being as the yeoman of his guard, waiting day and night, to protect him, for his protecting the nation, and them, and from all forcible assaults, and other perils; also, they be as his great and goodly ships, which hath purchased freedome, on the seas, and now lyes hovering up and down, as his castles, and strong forts of defence, as well as they, which stand upon the land, wherewith he doth prevent foreign hostility, represse inward tumults, and so keep himself, and the people, in peace and safety; likewise, as his judges, justices, sheriffs, constables, and other officers, watching, every hour and moment, in all shires, and counties, places, and corners of the nation, to represse outrages, and to maintain peace.

To maintain these laws, every good member hath the like benefit, as himself hath, for in fear of them, every person doth enjoy his life, and limbs in peace,

and

and is defended from the bloody-minded murderer, and man-queller, and the rage of the furious quarreller and fighter, and in fear of them, the houfekeeper refteth in peace, with his wife and family, under his own roof; the terror hereof doth often reftrain godlefle people, from committing perjuries, frauds, and deceits, and impudent, and fhamelefle men, to wreft from others, by bribery, extortion, or oppreffion.

And divers there be, who neither by the laws of God, of nature, or reafon, will be bridled, and reduced to vertue, yet by the penalties, and fear of our capital, and criminal laws, do yeeld to be curbed.

And we fhould now obferve, with what care, our fore-fathers, had, from one age to another, and what ordinances they eftablifhed, in parliament, that feveral penal, criminal, and capital laws, and ftatutes, fhould be read, or proclaimed, in churches, in fairs, in markets, at the general affizes, and quarter-feffions, of every county, at leets, and law-dayes, and in every inns of court, and chancery, and how the fame is continued, and put in practice, to the intent, that the fame laws, and the penalties thereof, fhould be heard, learned, known, and underftood, by all forts of perfons, willing to perceive, and apprehend the fame.

Charter-law is not fo, but like the foul fpirit in the air, ftill ranging, never at reft, nor will let others take any, never feen, but heard in every corner, ftriking at the pure law, to advance itfelf, it forces people to a kind of an order, in a town, and the whole nation, to a diforder.

The chiefeft reafon, why I give a recital of the penal laws, is, that the ignorant may fee how well they are provided for, and not to be left blind, and only being inftructed by the extortioner himfelf, what they muft pay, for fees, &c. (but that they may know themfelves) and to remedy themfelves, when offended, for fuch oppreffors would difcover no more, for safety of their purses, or bodies, then care was taken formerly, for others souls, when it was ordained, that the bibles should be in latine, and not in english, as appears, by statute the 34. of Henry 8. Several persons restrained from reading the bible, in english, &c. to keep them in ignorance, &c.

CHAP. LVIII.

The oath of an attorney at law.

(A) YOU shall do no falshood, nor consent to any, to be done in the court, and if you know of any, to be done, you shall give knowledge thereof, unto my lord chief justice, or other his brethren, that it may be reformed; you shall delay no man, for lucre, or malice; you shall increase no fees, but shall be contented with the old fees, accustomed; you shall plead no foreign plea, nor suffer no foreign suits, unlawfully, to hurt any man, but such, as shall stand, with order of the law, and your conscience; you shall seal all such profes, as you shall sue out of the court, with the seal thereof, and so the kings majesty, and my lord chief justice, discharge for the same; yee shall not wittingly, nor willingly sue, nor procure to be sued, any false suits, nor give aid, nor consent to the same, in pain to be expulsed from the court, for ever; and furthermore, you shall use yourself, in the office of an attorney, within the court, according to your learning and discretion. So help you God. See stat. 3. k. James, 7.

The oath of an under-sheriffe, bayliffe of franchises, deputies, and clerks of sheriffes, and under-sheriffes. Stat. 27. Eliz. 12.

(B) I (A.B) shall not use, or exercise, the office of under-sheriffe, corruptly, during the time I shall remain therein.

Neither shall, or will except, rejoyce, or take by any colour, means, or device whatsoever, or consent, to the taking of any manner of fee, or reward, of any manner of person, or persons, for the impanielling, or returning of any inquest jury, or tales, in any court of record, for the queen,* or between party and party, above two shillings, or the value thereof, or such fees, as are allowed, and appointed, for the same, by the lawes, and statutes of this realm.

But will, according to my power, truly and indifferently, with convenient speed, impanel all jurors, and return all such writ, or writs,* touching the same, as shall appertain to be done, by my duty, or office, during the time I shall remain in the said office. So help me God, and by the contents of this book.

The reason I write these oaths is, that perjury may the better appear to be punished, in officers, as well as others.

The oath of a jury.

(c) You shall truly enquire, and due presentment make, of all such things as you are charged withall, on the lord protectors behalf, the lord protectors council, your own, and your fellows; you shall well and truly keep, and in all other things, the truth present. So help you God, &c.

The oath of those, that give evidence to a jury, upon an indictment.

(D) The evidence you shall give, to the enquest, upon this bill, shall be the truth, the whole truth, and

and nothing but the truth; and you shall not let so to do, for malice, hatred, or evil will; nor for meed, dread, favor, or affection. So help you God, and the holy contents of this book.

CHAP. LIX.

King Charles his oath, at his coronation, with his hand upon the bible, at the altar.

(A) SIR, will you grant and keep, and by your oath, confirm to the people of England, their lawes and cuftoms, to them granted, by the kings of England, your lawfull and religious predeceffors, and namely, the lawes, cuftomes, and franchizes, granted to the clergy, and to the people, by the king, St. Edward, your predeceffor, according, and conformable to the laws of God, and profeffion of the gofpel, eftablifhed in this kingdom, and agreeing to the prerogatives, of the kings thereof, and to the antient cuftoms of this realm?

Refponf. I grant, and promife to keep.

Sir, will you keep peace, and agreement, intirely, according to your power, both to God, the holy church, the clergy, and the people?

Refponf. I will keep it.

Sir, will you, to your power, caufe law, juftice, and mercy, in difcretion and truth, to be executed, in all your judgements?

Refponf. I will.

Sir, will you grant, to hold and keep, the laws, and rightfull cuftoms,* which the commonalty of your kingdom have, and to defend, and uphold them, to the honor of God, fo much as in you lieth?

Refponf. I grant, and promife fo to do, and fhall obferve and keep. So God me help, and the contents of this book.

King John's oath, and fealty, to the Pope Innocentius, an. Dom. 1213.

(B) JOHN, by the grace of God, king of England, France, and Ireland, from this hour forward, shall be faithful to God,* and to St. Peter, and to the church of Rome, and to my lord, pope Innocentius, and to his successors, lawfully entering; I shall not be in word, and deed, in consent, or counsel, that they should loose life, or member, or be apprehended in evill manner; their loss, if I may know it, I shall impeach, and stay, so far as I shall be able, or else, so shortly as I can, I shall signifie unto them, and declare the same, unto you the councill, which they shall commit unto me, by themselves, their messengers, and their letters; I shall keep secretly, and not utter to any man, to their hurt, to my knowledge, the patrimony of St. Peter, and especially, the kingdom of England, and Ireland, and I shall endeavour, myself to defend, against all men, to my power. So help me God, and the holy evangelist, amen. See his reassignation of the liberties, after this oath, to the barons, of the liberties of England, in chap. 1. (K).

* It was time.

CHAP. LX.

The oath of a mayor of a corporation.

(A) YOU shall swear, that you well, and truly, shall serve the keepers, of the liberties of England, by authority of parliament, and the commonwealth, in the office of a mayor, and as mayor, of this town, and borough of Newcastle, for, and during, the space of one whole year, now next coming, and you shall minister equal justice, as well to the poor, as rich,* to the beſt of your cunning, wit, and power, and you ſhall procure ſuch things, to be done, as may honeſtly, and juſtly, be to the profit, and commodity of the corporation, of this town, and alſo, ſhall indeavor yourſelf, to the utmoſt of your power, to ſee all hereſies, treaſons, fellonies, and all other treſpaſſes, miſdemeanors,* and offences, whatſoever, to be committed,* within this town, and borough, during the time of your office, to be repreſſed; reformed, and amended,* and the offenders duly puniſhed, according to the law;* and finally, you ſhall ſupport, uphold, and maintain the commonwealth, within this town preſcribed, cuſtomes, rights, liberties, juriſdictions, franchizes, compoſitions, and all lawful ordinances, of this town, and borough,* and as concerning all other things, appertaining to your office, you ſhall therein, faithfully, and uprightly behave yourſelf, for the moſt quietneſs,* benefit, worſhip, honeſty, and credit of this town, and of the inhabitants thereof. So help you God.

The oath of burgeſſes of corporation.

(B) YOU ſhall ſwear, that you well, and truly, ſhall ſerve the keepers, of the liberties of England, by authority of parliament, and the inhabitants of this town, and borough of this town, as one of the burgeſſes of this town, and ſhall miniſter equall juſtice, to poor and rich, after the beſt of your cunning, wit, and power, and alſo, ſhall well, and truly obſerve, perform, fulfill, and keep, all ſuch good orders, rules, and compoſitions, as are, or ſhall be made, ordered, or eſtabliſhed, by the common council, of this town, for the good government thereof, in all things, to you appertaining, and you ſhall not utter, or diſcloſe any counſel, or ſecret thing, or matter, touching the fellowſhip, or corporation of this town, whereby, any prejudice, loſs, lofs, hindrance, or flander, fhall, or may arife, grow, or be, to the fame corporation, but you fhall, in things, belonging to the fellowfhip, or corporation of this town, faithfully, honeftly,* and indifferently, behave yourfelf, for the moft benefit, and honefty of this town, and the inhabitants thereof. So help you God.

The fame oath is for the aldermen.

Where the ftars are in the lines there will appear breaches.

CHAP. LXI.

The oath of a fheriff.

(A) YOU fhall fwear, that you fhall well, and truly, ferve the keepers, of the liberties of England, by authority of parliament, in the office of a fheriff, of the county of N. and do the keepers of the liberties of England profits, in all that belongeth you to do, by way of your office, as far forth, as you may, or can.

Yee fhall truly keep the keepers, &c. and all that belongeth to them ; ye fhall not affent to decreafe, to leffen, nor to concealment, of any of their rights, or franchizes, and whenfoever yee fhall have knowledge, that their rights be concealed, or withdrawn, be it in lands, rents, franchizes, or fuits, or any other thing, ye fhall do your true power, to make them be reftored to them again, and if ye may not do it, ye fhall certifie them thereof, fuch as you know for certain, will fay unto them; ye fhall not refpect their debts, for any gift, or favour, when ye may raife them, without grievance to the debtor;

T 2   ye fhall ye ſhall truly, and righteouſly, treat the people of your ſheriffwick, and do right well, to poor, as to rich, in all, that belongs to your office.

Ye ſhall do no wrong, to any man, for any gift, or other beheſt, or promiſe of goods; for favor, nor hate, ye ſhall diſturb no mans right; ye ſhall acquit, at the exchequer, all thoſe, of whom ye ſhall any thing receive, of the keepers, &c. debts; ye ſkall nothing take, whereby the keepers, &c. may looſe, or that right may be letten, or diſturbed, or the keepers, &c. debt delaid; ye ſhall truly receive, and truly ſerve the keepers, &c. writs as far forth, as it ſhall be in your cunning; ye ſhall not have, to be your under ſheriff, any of the ſheriffs clerks, of the laſt years paſſed; ye ſhall take no bayliff, into your ſervice, but ſuch, as you will anſwer for; ye ſhall make, each of your bailiffs, make ſuch oath, as you make yourſelf, in that that belongeth to their occupation; ye ſhall receive no writs, by you, nor any of yours, unſealed, nor any ſealed, under the ſeal of any juſtice, ſave of juſtices of Eyre, or juſtices, aſſigned in the ſame ſhire, where you be ſheriff in, or other juſtices, having power, or authority, to make any writs unto you, by the law of the land.

You ſhall make your bayliffs, of the true, and ſufficient men in the country; ye ſhall be dwelling, in your own proper perſon, within your bayliwick, for the time; you ſhall be in the ſame office, except you ſhall be licenſed, by the keepers, &c. you ſhall not let your ſheriffwick, nor any bayliwick thereof, to farm, to any man; ye ſhall truly ſet, and return, reaſonable, and due luſes, of them, that be within your bayliwick, after their eſtate and behaviour, and make your pannel yourſelf, of ſuch perſons, as be moſt meet, moſt ſufficient, and not ſuſpect, nor procured, as it is ordained, in the ſtatute, and over this, in eſchewing, and reſtraining of the robberies, manſlaughters, and other manifold grievous offences, that be done daily, by ſuch, as name themſelves
ſouldiers,

HENRY III.

fouldiers, and by other vagrants, by which increafe, in multitude, and number, fo that the good people may not fafely ride, nor go, to do fuch things, as they have to do, to their intollerable hurt, and hindrance; ye fhall truly, and effectually, with all diligence poffible, to your power, execute the ftatute of Winchefter, for vaggabonds; all thefe things, ye fhall well, and truly obferve, and keep. So help you God.

It is the judgement of learned councel, that fheriffs may be indicted, for perjury, by wilful neglect of their duty, as other perfons, wilfully, or procuringly, perjures themfelves, &c.

KING HENRY THE THIRD,

Was crouned, at the age of 9 yeres, the 28. October, 1216, he raigned 56 yeres, and 20 daies, dyed, the 16. November, 1272, lyeth buried, at Weftminfter.

None to be condemned, but by the judgment of the law.

STAT. ninth year of his reign, chap. 29. in parliament, enacts, that no free-man fhall be taken, or imprifoned, or be diffeazed, of his free-hold, liberties, or free cuftomes, or pafs upon him, or condemn him, but by lawful judgement of his equals, or by the law of the land; we will not fell to no man, we will not defer to any man, either juftice, or right. Reg. fo. 186. Coke, Pla. 456. Dyer, fo. 104. Coke, lib. 5. fo. 64. lib. 10. fo. 74. lib. 11. fo. 99. ftat. 2. Edw. 3. 8. 5. Edw. 3. 9. 14. Edw. 3. 14. 28. Edw. 3. 3. 11. Rich. 2. 19. 3. Carol. Pet. of right. See chap. 38. (A.C).

Bakers,

Bakers, and brewers, faulty, to be punished.

Stat. 51. year of his reign, 1266, enacts, that if any baker, or brewer, be convict, becaufe he hath not obferved the affize, of bread and ale, for the firft, fecond, and third time, he fhall be amerced, according to his offence, but if he amend not, then to fuffer punifhment of body, the. baker, to the pillory, and brewer, to the tumbrel, which fhall not be remitted, for gold nor filver, and impowres ale cunners, in every town, &c. every baker, to fet his own mark, on his bread. See chap. 49. (c).

KING HENRY THE FOURTH,

Born at Bollingbroke, in the countie of Lincolne, began his raigne, the 26. of September, 1399, raigned 13 yeares, and 6 monetbs, and died, in an. Dom. 1413, of the age of 46 yeares, buried, at Canterbury.

Juftice fhall be done in England.

STAT. firft year of his reign, chapter the firft, enacts the confirmation, of the liberties of England, and all ftatutes, not repealed ; peace fhall be maintained, and juftice fhall be done, to all men.

Sheriffes fhall not let their county to farm.

Stat. the fourth year of his reign, chapter. the fifth, enacted, that every fheriff, in England, fhall abide in proper perfon, within his bayliwick, for the time, he fhall be fuch officer, and that, he fhall not let his bayliwick, to farm, to any man, for the time, that he occupieth, fuch office, and that the faid

fheriffe

HENRY IV.

HENRY V.

ſheriffe, be ſworn, from time to time, to do the ſame, in ſpecial, amongſt other articles, compriſed, in the oath of ſheriffs. Stat. 23. Hen. 6. 10.

KING HENRY THE FIFTH.

Began his raigne, the 20. of March, was crouned, at Weſtminſter, the 9. of Aprill, 1413. He raigned 9 yeares, 2 months, died, in the caſtel of Boyes, neer Paris, the 13. of Auguſt, 1422, buried, at Weſt-minſter.

Coals to pay, two pence, per chaldron, cuſtome, and keels, to be meaſured.

(A) STAT. the ninth year of his reign, chap. 9. 10. it was enacted, the king ſhould have two pence, of every chalder of coals, of unfranchized men, in the river, and port, at Newcaſtle upon Tyne, as cuſtomes, and, for the better knowledge of ſuch cuſtomes, ordains, that all keels, or boats, which carried coals, to ſhips, ſhould be, of the juſt burden of twenty chaldron of coals. Notwithſtanding this act, the Newcaſtle men, made the keels, to carry, ſome, two, and ſome, three and twenty, to wrong the king, of his cuſtomes, which great cheat, was proved in parliament, where they enacted, to prevent ſuch like, for the future, that ſworn commiſſioners, ſhould mark all keels, and other veſſels, carrying coals, to ſhips, upon pain of forfeiture, of keel and coals. See chap. 9. (A), 11. chap. (1).

KING HENRY THE SIXTH,

Of the age of 8 moneths, began his raigne, the 1. of September, 1422, crowned, at Weſtminſter, the 6. of November, 1429, afterward, crowned, at Paris, 7. September, 1431, raigned 38 yeares, 6 moneths, 4 dayes, buried, at Winſore.

Puniſhments of cuſtomers, for not clearing ſhips.

(A) STAT. the eleventh year of his reign, chap, 15. enacted, that, for as much as the cuſtomers, and controlers, in the kings ports, do not write any warrants, in diſcharge of merchants, of their merchandizes, by them ſhewed, and duely cuſtomed, tranſported, or imported, the ſame cuſtomers, and controlers, do imbezel the kings cuſtomes, and the merchants be greatly hindred, becauſe that the warrants might plainly ſhew, and declare their due cuſtome, when they be often, and unduly impeached, in the kings exchequor; in conſideration of the ſaid deceits, it was enacted, that the ſaid cuſtomers, and controlers, ſhall write, and deliver, ſufficient warrants, ſealed, with the ſeal of their office, to that end ordained, to the ſaid merchants, not any thing to be given for the ſame, but their due cuſtome; and, that in caſe any cuſtomer, or controler, do the contrary, then the merchant may have an action, by vertue of this ordinance, to purſue every cuſtomer, or controler, that doth the contrary, in every court of record, and being thereof attainted, ſhall forfeit, to the king, for every default, ten pounds, and to the merchant grieved, that ſueth, five pound. 11. Hen. 6. 15. See chap. 45. (E).

The great danger, occaſioned by ſmall riots.

(B) In the 37. year of his reign, began ſuch riots, routs, and unlawful aſſemblies, that it produced a

worſe

HENRY VI.

worfe effect, then in king Richard the feconds dayes, which was occafioned, between a yeoman of the guard, and a ferving man, of the earle of Warwick, which fo far increafed, not being timely prevented, that it proved the root of many a woful tragedy, brought to death the duke of York, who was proclaimed fucceffor to the crown; the king, prince Edward his fon, all, or moft of the peers of the land deftroyed, by fidings, and, at leaft, fix and thirty thoufand of the common people, cut off, at one battel, at Toughton, in Yorkfhire, the king, queen, and prince, put to flight, to Barwick. See Richard the fecond, what was done. See chapter 37. (A), 3. Hen. 6. See Rich. 2. (E).

Sheriffs fees ; none of his officers fhall be returned, upon inquefts, letting to bayl, &c.

(c) Stat. 23. Hen. the fixth, chapter 10. The king, confidering the great perjury, extortion, and oppreffion, which be, and have been, in his realm, by his fheriffes, under-fheriffs, and their clerks, coroners, ftewards of franchizes, bayliffs, and keepers of prifons, and other officers, in divers counties of this realm, have ordained, by the authority aforefaid, in efchewing of all fuch perjury, extortion, and oppreffion, and, that becaufe the fheriffe of every county, is a great, and neceffary officer, in the commonwealth, and ufed, as a fpecial inftrument, to the furtherance of juftice, in all fuits, purfued at the common-law, and his fervice is employed, in the beginning, profecuting, and ending, of the moft of them, therefore, as the law, hath alwayes, had a fpecial regard of him, and forefeen, that he fhall be a man of wifdome, of worth, of credit, countenance, and ability, (this is not William Fenwick, of North Riding, in Northumberland, for he derogates from them all) and that he fhall be allowed, a convenient ftipend, and falary, for his pains, in moft cafes, fo

U   doth

doth fhe carry a vigilant, and watchful eye, upon him, and his inferiour officers, or fubftitutes, knowing what grievous oppreffions might enfue, if fhe fhould leave a man of his authority, and neceffary imployment, at liberty, to dive, at his pleafure, into other mens purfe, and to take what he would, (as William Fenwick doth) therefore, fhe hath reftrained him, his under fheriffe, bayliffe of franchizes, and other bayliffes, (moft of which are forefworn) within certain lifts, and affigned them, what they fhall take for arrefts, attachments, mainprizes, letting to bail, and ferving of executions, which, if any of them do exceed, he fhall forfeit, forty pound a time, and fhall be adjudged an extortioner, in which faid ftatute, it is enacted, that no fheriffe, under-fheriffe, or any bayliffe, by occafion, or under colour of his office, fhall take any other thing, by themfelves, or any other perfon, to their ufe, or to their profit, of any perfon, by any of them arrefted, or attached, nor of any other for them, for the omitting of any arreft, or attachment, to be made, by their bodies, or of any perfon, by any of them, by force, or colour of their office, arrefted, or attached, for fine, fee, mainprize, letting to bail, or, for fhewing any cafe, or favour, to any fuch perfon, fo arrefted, for their reward, or profit, but fuch as follows; the fheriffe, twenty-pence, the bayliffe, which maketh the arreft, or attachment, four pence, the gaoler, if the prifoner be committed to his ward, four pence; for making of a return, or paniel, and for the copy of a paniel, four-pence; no bond to be made, by them, under colour of their office, but onely to themfelves, for the appearance of any prifoner, at the day prefcribed, and what bond is otherwife, is void; and he fhall take no more, for making fuch obligation, warrant, or precept, by him to be made, but four pence; and all fheriffes, under-fheriffes, clerks, bayliffes, gaolers, coroners, ftewards, bayliffes of franchizes, or any other officer, or minifters, which

which doth, contrary to the aforesaid ordinances, in any point of the same, shall lose, to the party, in this behalf endamaged, or grieved, his treble damages, and shall forfeit, forty pounds, at every time, that any do the contrary, in any point of the same, whereof the king shall have the one half, to be imployed, only to the use of his house, and the other, to the party, that will sue for the same, by bill, plaint, &c.

I shall lay open the excessive fees, extorted by the sheriffs of Northumberland, against the law, viz.

	l.	s.	d.
Return a tales	0	6	0
For allowance of a pony	0	9	2
For allowance of a writ, false judgement	0	16	6
Upon execution granting out	0	15	0
And all upon the defendant, after execution	1	11	6
For breaking open an original proces	0	2	6
For the warrant thereof	0	0	6
Bayliffs, for the arrest from the plaintiff	0	1	0
From the party arrested	0	1	8
To file bayl above, and taking the declaration	0	8	0

This is costly law.
This justice is both bought and sold, &c.
A bill of indictment, before a judge, would reduce these, &c.

The form of an indictment, for sheriffs.

(D) London ss. The jurors, for the lord protector, of the commonwealth of England, Scotland, and Ireland, &c. upon their oaths, do present, that John Butler, of London, sheriffe, the 20th. day of August, in the year of our Lord God, 1652, being then sheriffe, and keeper of the prison, of the Newgate, in London, the day, and year aforesaid, did, by force, or colour of his said office, as sheriffe, and keeper of the said prison, unlawfully, and extortionously exact, and take of one John Cuthberton, then, and there, being arrested, and imprisoned in the said prison, under the custody of the said sheriff, at the suit of John Roe, the sum of six shillings and eight pence, for the fee of the said sheriffe, and keeper, for the custody of the said John, in the said prison, from the 20. day of the month of May, in the year aforesaid, until the 20. day of August, then next following, to the great damage of the said John, and to the evill example of others, in the like case offending, and contrary to the form of the statute, in such case made, and provided, and against the public peace. See chap. 58. (c), (d), (b), stat. 23. Hen. 8. 3.

KING HENRY THE SEVENTH,

Began his raigne, the 22. of June, 1485, and was crowned, at Westminster, the 30. of October. He raigned 25 yeares, and 8 monthes, and died, the 22. of April, lieth buried, at Westminster.

STAT. 3. Hen. 7. chap. 1. * It is enacted, if any coroner be remisse, and maketh not inquisition upon the view of the body dead, and certifie not, according to his office, it is ordained, that he shall, for every default, forfeit five pounds. See chap. 10. (o.p), chap. 48. 29. 49.

Weights and measures, &c.

Stat. 11. Hen. 7. chap. 4. For as much, as many grievances have been set forth, unto this present parlament, of the great fraud, and deceit, in measures,

HENRY VII.

meafures, and weights, for remedy whereof, it is ordained, and enacted, that, to the knights, and citizens, of every fhire, and city, affembled, in, this prefent parlament, barons of the five ports, and certain burgeffes, of burrough towns, ere they depart, from this prefent parliament, be delivered, one, of every weight, and meafure, which now is made of brafs, for the good of the fubject, according to the kings ftandard, of his exchequer, of weights, and meafures, and that they fhall caufe all common weights, and meafures, to be as abovefaid, and all fuch as prove defective, then fuch weights and meafures, fhall be broken and burnt, and the party pay twenty fhillings, and be fet in the pillory; the quarter of corn, to be eight bufhels, raifed, and ftruck, and fourteen pound, to the ftone of wool, &c. and water meafure, to be five pecks on fhip board, according to the ftandard, &c. See chap. 49, (c).

No ordinance to be made by corporations, &c.

By act of parlament, 19. Hen. 7. 7. That mafters, wardens, and people of guilds, fraternities, and of other companies corporate, oftentimes, by colour of rule, and governance, to them granted by charter, and letters pattents, made amongft themfelves, many unlawfull, and unwarrantable ordinances, as well in prizes of wages, as other things, for their own fingular profit, and to the common hurt, and damage of the people, be it enacted, and it is hereby enacted, that no fuch mafter, wardens, nor companies*, make, nor ufe, any ordinance, in difheritance, nor diminition, of the prerogative of the king, nor of others,* nor againft the common profit of the people, nor none other ordinance of charge, except it were firft difcuft, ufed, and and proved, by good advice of the juftices of peace, or the chief governors of cities, and before them, entered upon

on record, and that upon pain, to loofe, and forfeit the force, and effect of all the articles, in their faid letters pattents, and charters contained, concerning the fame, and over that, to pay ten pounds to the king, for every ordinance, that any of them made, or ufed, to the contrary, the fame ordinance to indure, at the kings pleafure, which act was then expired, and fince the expiration of the fame, many ordinances have been made, by many private bodies, within divers cities, towns, and burroughs, contrary to the kings prerogative, his laws, and the common weal of his fubjects; be it therefore enacted, that no mafters, wardens, and fellowfhip of crafts, or myfteries, nor of any rulers of guilds, or fraternities,* take upon them, to make any acts, or ordinances, nor to execute any, by them heretofore made, in difhertion, or diminition of the prerogative of the king, nor of other, nor againft the common profit of the people, except the faid acts, and ordinances, be examined, and approved by the chancellor, treafurer of England, or chief juftices, of either benches, or three of them, or before both the juftices of affizes, in their circuit, in the fhire, where fuch acts, or ordinances be made, upon pain of forfeiture of forty pounds, for every time they doe to the contrary; and over that, it is enacted, that none of the fame bodies corporate, take upon them, to make any acts, or ordinances, to reftrain* any perfon, or perfons, to fue to the king, or any of his courts, for due remedy, to be had in their caufes, nor put, nor execute any penalty, or punifhment, upon any of them, for any fuch fuit to be made, upon pain of forfeiture of forty pounds, for every time, that they do to the contrary. See chap. 39. (A), 30. (D), 43. (D), and chap. 10. (G).

This ftatute will prove offenfive to the free hoaftmen, and the charter of the admiralty, if well profecuted, and pay them for all the wrongs done.

KING

HENRY VIII.

KING HENRY THE EIGHTH,

Was borne, at Greenwich, entered his raigne, being 18 yeares of age, the 22. Aprill, 1509, was crouned, at Westminster, the 25. of June following. He raigned 37 yeares, and 9 months, died, the 28. of June, buried, at Winsor.

(A) STAT. 21. Hen. 8. chap. 18. In the vacancy of the sea of Durham, cardinal Wolsey being dead, and no knights, nor burgesses, in parlament, for Durham, and Northumberland, then, the mayor, and burgesses of Newcastle, knowing there could be no opposition, petitioned the king, and parlament, for that, whereas the mayor, burgesses, and commonalty of that town, having been faithfull subjects, and held, in fee, from his progenitors, that town, port, and haven of the river of Tine, thereunto belonging, and of all ground,* which the water covered, within the said river of Tine, from the mouth of the said river, called Sparhawke, and to Headwin streams, in their demean, as of fee, in right of the crown, and that all merchandizes, carryed by any ship, or vessell, into that port, or carried out, used to be discharged, and loaden, only, at that town, by which means, the customs, subsidies, and tole, were received there, for his majesties use, 500l. per annum, and that by reason of those liberties, and franchizes, that town hath been well replenished, and maintained, and able to furnish his majesty, with four hundred marriners for the war, and by reason of several great personages, as well spiritual, as temporal, having lands adjoyning to the said river, have loaden and unloaden ships, with several merchandizes, and paid no customs, to the utter undoing of the town, and the great dishertion of your highness, and minishment to your customs, and that divers weyers, and fish-gates, were erected in the said river, by

means

means whereof great sand-beds, and gravel heaps, be grown, and cast up, in the said river, that within few years to come, no ship of good burthen, or weight,* shall be able to come up to the town, to the inestimable hurt of the countries, thereunto adjoyning, and to the damage of your realm,* especially, to all persons needing sea coals, which be onely conveyed, from the said port, and no where else, to be shipped, or had, but there.

In consideration whereof, may it please your majestie, out of your bounden grace, with the assent of your lords, spiritual and temporal, and the commons, in parlament, to enact, ordain, and establish, that from henceforth, any merchant, or merchants, or any other person, or persons, shall not ship, load, or unload, any merchandize, or other wares of goods, to be sold here, between the said place, called Sparhawke, and Headwin streams, (being fourteen miles in length) but onely at Newcastle, upon pain of forfeiture, of all such goods, and wares, and merchandizes, to the king.

And for the mayor, and burgesses, to pull down all weires, goares, and engins, which was granted by the said statute, provided alwaies this act be not prejudicial to any person, or persons, being the kings subjects, for building, shipping, loading, or unloading, any salt, or fish, within the said river, and port, or to any of them, or to any other persons, repairing to the said port, with ships and merchandizes, for selling, or buying of any merchandizes, or wares, needful for victualing, and amending of the said ships,* at the time of their being in the said port, this act, or any thing comprised in the same, notwithstanding. See chap. 50. (c).

A table of fees, for customs, toles, &c. in towns.

(D) Stat. 22. Hen. 8. chap. 8. Be it enacted, that every city, borough, and town corporate, their officer

cer shall set up, or cause a table, in open place, of, and for the certainty of all such, and every duty, of every such custom, tole, and duty, or sum of money, of such wares and merchandizes, to be demanded, or required, as above rehearsed, shall, and may plainly appear to be declared, to the intent, that nothing be exacted, otherwise, than in old time hath been used, and accustomed, upon pain of each city, five pound, and every corporation, forty shillings, for every month, that the said table shall fail to be set up, the moyety to the king, and the other to the party, that will sue for the same, by writ, bill, plaint, or information, in which the defendant shall have no assoyn, wager of law, nor protection of law, allowed. See chap. 44. (E).

A commission of sewers, &c.

(c) Stat. 23. Hen. 8. chap. 5. The king, considering the absolute necessity, of granting a general act, for commissioners of sewers, to be directed, in all parts of his realm, for the advancing of the commonwealth, and commodity of this his realm, and likewise, considering the daily great damages, and losses, which have happened in many parts of the nation, in the decay, and spoil of rivers, to the inestimable damages of the commonwealth, which do daily increase; for remedy whereof, it is enacted, that there be commissioners of suers, and other premises, directed, in all parts, from time to time, where and when need shall require, to such substantial, and indifferent persons, as shall be named by the lord chancellor, and lord treasurer of England, and the two chief justices, for the time being, or by three of them, whereof the lord chancellor to be one.

The commissioners to be residing, in the respective countie, where the commission is directed, (which said commissioners, will preserve the said river) having power given them, to conſtitute and ordain laws, ordinances, and decrees, and to repeal, reform, and amend, as need ſhall require, any defects.

Alſo, to pull down any newſances, incroachments, or the like, erected in the ſaid rivers, and to cauſe buildings of wharfs, for the good of the ſame, and power, to rate, and tax any perſon whatſoever, towards the charge, for the good of the ſaid rivers, or having ſpoyled the ſame, to ſeize his, or their lands, tenements, goods, and chattels, for the ſaid taxes, and to diſpoſe of the ſame, by ſail, leaſe, or otherwiſe, ſix commiſſioners being preſent, and every commiſſioner is to have four ſhillings a day, when they ſit, and the clerk, two ſhillings a day, out of the taxes. I refer the reſt of this power, to the relation of theſe ſtatutes following. 3. Edw. 6. 9. 13. Eliz. 9. See 34. chap. (c), 35. (a.b).

An attaint againſt a jury.

(d) Stat. 23. Hen. 8. chap. 3. The law having firſt uſed all good devices to cauſe ſheriffs, under-ſheriffs, bayliffs of liberties, coroners, and all others authorized to return, and impannel juries, to be indifferent, and to return the ſaid jurors, and juries, without all partiallity, and that they ſhall be no furtherers, maintainers, nor aſſiſters to perjury, ſubordination, or embracery, and alſo having provided, that all thoſe jurors, which be ſo returned upon inqueſts, and to try inqueſts, and to try iſſues between party and party, may again, one by one, be ſifted, tryed, and examined, whether they ſtanding unſworn, be indifferent, or not; ſhe doth then expect from thoſe jurors, *veridictum*, a true tale, that is to ſay, a true verdict, or preſentment, of ſuch things as be given them, in charge, according to their evidence, but if the ſame jurors, will decline from truth, and make a falſe preſentment, contrary to their evidence,* then, it is not to be tearmed
veredictum,

veredictum, but *perjurium*, and it will be returned to them, as *maledictum*, for by the common-law, they being attainted, by the verdict of four and twenty other jurors, shall receive a curled, and villainous judgement; therefore, viz.

The said jurors, shall lose the freedom of the law, their wives, and children shall be thrust out of their houses, their houses shall be pulled down to the ground, their orchards, and gardens shall be subplanted, their trees shall be digged up by the roots, their meadows shall be eyred up, all their goods, and chattels, which they have at the time of the attaint brought, or at any time after, shall be forfeited to the king, the king shall have all the profit of their forfeited lands, during their lives, and they shall be committed to perpetuall prison, which judgement, was devised, and many years put in execution, to the intent, it might be known, how much the common-law did detest, and punish wilfull perjury, and falsehood, in those who she trusted, in place of justice, and from whom she accounted to receive truth. See *Poulton, Perjury*, (16). See chap. 58. (B.C.D,) stat. 23. Hen. 6. 10. (D).

To prevent spoyl in rivers by ballast.

(c) Stat. 34. Hen. 8. 9. The king, for the good and preservation of rivers, enacted, that what person, or persons, do cast, or unlade any ballast, rubbish, gravel, or other wreck out of any ship, crayer, or other vessels, being within any haven-road, channel, or river to any port, town, or other city, or borough, within this realm, but onely upon the land, above the full sea-mark, upon pain of forfiture of five pound a time, the one half to the king, the other, to the party discovering, that will sue for the same, by bill, plaint, or otherwise, no wager of law admitted, or any essoyn, or protection allowed.

This is a legal courfe, but Newcaftle acts not hereby, as you may fee, in chap. 34. (c), 35. (A.B), 12. chap. (6), 14. (B).

KING EDWARD THE FIRST.

Sheriffs punifhed for refufing bail.

(A) STAT. 3. Ed. 1. 15. King Edward the firft, for as much as fheriffs, and others, which have taken, and kept in prifon, perfons detected of felony, and incontinent, have let out, by plevyn, fuch as were not replevifable, and kept in perfons, fuch as were replevifable, becaufe they would win of the one party, and grieve the other, it is ordained, that if any fheriffe, or any other, which hath the keeping of prifons, let any go at large, by furety, that is not replevifable, and thereof be attainted, he fhall lofe his fee, and office, for ever, and if the under-fheriffe, conftable, or bayliff, of fuch who have fees, for keeping of prifons, do it, contrary to the will of his lord, or any other bayliff, being not of fee, they fhall have three years imprifonment, and make fine, at the kings pleafure, and if any man with-hold a prifoner replevifable, after that they have offered fufficient furety, he fhall pay a grievous amerciament to the king, and if he take any reward, for the deliverance of fuch, he fhall pay it double, to the prifoner, and alfo, fhall pay a grievous amerciament, to the king. See ftat. 27. Edw. 1. 3. ftat. 3. Hen. 7. 2. the firft and fecond Philip and Mary, 13. See 30. chap. (B), 37. chap. (A), 41. chap. (A).

Extortion

EDWARD I.

Extortion in officers.

(B) Stat. 3. Ed. 1. 26. The king ordains, that none of his officers shall commit extortion, neither sheriffe, nor other shall take reward, to do his office, but shall be paid, of that which they take of the king, and he that so doth, shall pay, or yeeld two times as much, and shall be punished, at the kings pleasure. See stat. 23. Hen. 6. 10.

Outrageous tole.

(c) Stat. 3. Edw. 1. 30. The king ordains, that such who takes outrageous tole, contrary to the common custome of the realm, in market towns, by the lord, then the franchizes of the said market, to be seized into the kings hand, and if it be in the kings town, which is let in the farm, the franchizes to be seized, in the kings hand, and if it be done, by a bayliffe, without consent of his lord, he shall restore double, and shall have forty dayes imprisonment; touching citizens, and burgesses, to whom the king granted murrage, to inclose their towns,* which takes such murrage, otherwise then it was granted unto them, and thereof be attainted, it is provided, that they shall lose their charter, or grant, for ever, and shall be grievously amerced, unto the king. (See 44. Edw. 3. fo. 20.) 43. Edw. 3. fo. 29. (Fit. N. B. fo. 94.). See 11. chap. (H), 44. (1), 49. (c), 48. (A).

Persons attached out of their liberty.

(D) Stat. 3. Ed. 1. 34. For as much as great men, and the bayliffs, and others, the kings officers onely excepted, unto whom special authority is given, which, at the complaint of some, are by their own authority attached, others passing through their jurisdictions with their goods, compelling them to
answer

answer afore them,* upon contract, covenants, and trespasses, out of their jurisdiction, where indeed they hold nothing of them, or within their franchizes, where their power is, in prejudice of the king, and his crown, and to the damage of the people, it is provided, that none, from henceforth, fo do, and if any do, he shall pay to him, that by his occasion shall be attached, his damage double, and shall be grievously amerced to the king. 3. Ed. 1. 16. See chap. 30. (B).

The penalties for procuring writs.

(E) Stat. 13. Edw. 1. 36. For as much as lords of courts, and others, that keeps courts, and stewards, intending to grieve their inferiors, where they have no lawful means so to do, procures others, to move matters against them, and to put in sureties, and other pledges, or to purchase writs, and at the suit of such plaintiffes, compels them to follow the county, hundred, wapentake, and other like courts, untill they have made fine with them, at their will; it is ordained, that it shall not be so used hereafter, and if any be attached, upon such false complaints, he shall replevy his distresse, so taken, and shall cause the matter to be brought afore the justice, before whom, if the sheriff, bayliff, or other lord, after that the party distrained, hath framed his complaint, will advow the distresse lawful, by reason of such complaints made unto them, and it be replied, that such complaints were moved maliciously, against the party, by the solicitation, or procurement of the sheriff, or other bayliffe, or lord, the same replication shall be admitted, and if they be convicted hereupon, they shall make fine to the king, and treble damages to the party grieved. See stat. 8. Eliz. 2.

No tax to be levied but by parliament, &c.

(F) Stat. 25. Edw. 1. 6. Be it enacted, that none shall be charged, by any charge, or impofition, nor be compelled to contribute to any tax, talledge, aid, or other like charge, not fet by common confent in parliament.

A writ called Ad quoddamum, to purchafe fairs, markets, &c.

(G) Stat. 27. Ed. 1. 1299. The king ordains, that if any perfon, or perfons, having a mind to obtain any liberties, fairs, markets, or the like, may have this writ out of chancery, called *Ad quoddamum*; if the inqueft paffe for them, they fhall have it, for remembrance of which thing, there is an indenture made, and divided into three parts, whereof one part remains in the chancery, another in the exchequor, and the third in the wardrop. Regift. fo. 247. Fitz. N. B. fo. 221. Raft. Pla. fo. 25. 32. See chap. 48. (A.B), 44. (1), 49. (A.G), 50. (A), 29. (A), 47. (A), 51. (A), 50. (C), and chap. 11. (I.K).

This writ, called a quo warranto, will dafh any charter a pecces exceeded.

(H) Stat. 30. Ed. 1. 1301. The king and his parliament, provided well for the weal of the nation, againft any indirect courfe, profecuted under colour of charter, grants, &c. either by not putting in execution, what is granted to corporations, or exceeding their powers, ordains this writ, whereby all men may have right, if they look after it, viz. The king to the fheriff, greeting, fummon by good fummons, &c. that they be before us, at &c. in our next coming, into the county aforefaid, or before our juftices of affize, when they fhall come into
thofe

thofe parts, to fhew, by what warrant they claim fuch liberties, and hold a view of frank pledge, in their mannor of &c. or by what warrant they have, to hold *Tholonium* (*tollis*) for them, and their heirs, and by what warrant they do fuch wrongs, &c.

This writ, is like twenty of the violenteft maftiffs, upon a fmall bear, tearing her all in peeces, they being unmuzled. There is great want of fuch bayting.

(I) Doctor Lamb, who was killed by a rude multitude, in London, and foon after buried, but by reafon a coroner did not view his dead body, &c. this writ was brought, by attorney general Noy, who voided their charter, and they were fined many thoufand pounds, and paid, &c.

(K) London-Derry, onely for exceeding their power, in their charter, were ferved the very like, &c.

This writ would do the like to Newcaftle, if' acted, for exceeding their powers, and not burying Mr. Snapes fon, one Gray, and William Rea, who were drowned in that river, as they are tyed to do by charter. See chap. 10. (O.P), and fee chap. 29. (A), 48. (B), 49. (Y).

No diftreffe without warrant.

(L) Stat. 34. Ed. 1. 2. The king ordains, that no officer of his, or his heirs, fhall take any corn, cattle, or any other goods whatever, from any perfon, without the good will, and affent of the party, to whom the goods belonged. See chap. 47. (A), 30. (B).

EDWARD II.

KING EDWARD THE SECOND,

Surnamed Carnarven, was crouned, at Weſtminſter, at the 22. yere of his age, the 24. of February, 1308. He raigned 19 yere, 6 monethes, was depoſed the 25. of Januarius, 1326. He was ſlayne in the caſtle of Barkley, in the 43. yere of his age.

Breaking of priſons.

(A) STAT. 1. Ed. 2. 1307. By the common-law of England, if a man had been impriſoned, and broke the priſon, he ſhould have been hanged, for what cauſe ſoever he had been impriſoned, yea, although it had been but for treſpaſs, which great enormity was redreſſed, by this ſtatute of 1. Edw. 2. intituled, *De frangentibus priſonam*, the words where be theſe, touching priſoners breaking of priſon, our lord the king, doth will and command, that none, which from henceforth do break priſon, ſhall have judgement of life, and member, for the breaking of priſon onely, except the cauſe for the which he was taken, and impriſoned, doth require ſuch judgement, if he ſhould have been convicted thereof, according to the law, and cuſtom of the realm, though in times paſt, it hath been otherwiſe uſed, and therefore it is to be conſidered, who is a priſoner, and what is breaking of priſon. According to the meaning of the aforeſaid ſtatute, every perſon, who is under arreſt, for felony, is a priſoner, as well being out of the goal, as within, ſo that if he be but in the ſtocks, in the ſtreet, or out of the ſtocks, in the poſſeſſion of any, that hath arreſted him, and doth make an eſcape, that is a breaking of priſon, in the priſoner, for impriſonment is none other, but a reſtraint of liberty. Raſt. pla. fo. 247. 340. Kil. fo. 87. Dyer, fo. 99. Fitz. Coron. 134. Bro. Coron. 79.

Unſufficient Sheriffs.

(B) Stat. 9. Edw. 2. 1315. The king, receiving great complaints, from the great men, and people in parliament, throughout the whole realm, perceived great damage done to him, and great oppreſſion, and diſheritances to his people, by reaſon of unſufficient ſheriffs, and bailiffs; the king, reſolved to prevent ſuch evil oppreſſions, and diſheritances, by the aſſent of his prelates, barons, &c. enacted, that the ſheriffs, ſhall have ſufficient land, within the ſame ſhire, to anſwer the king, and his people, and to attend his office, and if any ſheriffs, or hundreders, be unſufficient, ſhall be removed,* and others, more convenient, put in their place; that none ſhall farm his land; that writs, ſent to the ſheriffs, ſhall be executed by the hundreders, ſworn and known; they to be ſuch——as have land, to anſwer, and not by others, ſo that the people may know to whom to ſue, ſuch execution, ſaving always the returns of the writs, to them that have them, or ought to have them.

The king, by his prerogative, ſhall have the wreck of the ſea.

(c) Stat. 17. Edw. 2. 11. It is enacted, that the king ſhall have the wreck of the ſea, throughout the realm, whales, and great ſturgeon, taken in the ſea, or elſewhere, within the realm, except in certain places privileged by the king. See ſtat. 3. Edw. 1. 4. Raſt. pla. fo. 611. Co. lib. fo. 106. 108. 1. Hen. 7. fo. 23. 11. Hen. 4. fo. 16. 9. Hen. 7. fo. 20. 35. Hen. 6. fo. 27. See chap. 10. (s), 30. (A), 29. (D), 30. (c).

The

The king shall have all felons goods.

(D) Stat. 17. Ed. 2. 16. Be it enacted, the king shall have the goods of all felons, attainted, and fugitives, wherefoever they be found, and if they have freehold, then it shall be forthwith taken into the kings hands, and the king shall have all profits of the same, by one year, and one day, and the land shall be wasted, and destroyed, the houses, woods, and gardens, and all manner of things, belonging to the same, excepting men of certain places, privileged by the king therefore, and after he hath had the year and the day, and the waste, then the land shall be restored to the chief lord of the same fee, unless that he fine before with the king, for the year and the day, and the waste; nevertheless, it is used in the county of Glocester, by custome, that after one year and a day, the lands, and tenements of fellons shall revert, and be restored to the next heir, to whom it ought to have descended, if the fellony had not been done, and in Kent, the custome is gavel kind, the father to the bow, and the son to the plow: All heirs male shall divide their inheritance, and likewife women, but women shall not make partition with men, and a woman, after the death of her husband, shall be endowed of the moiety, and if she commit fornication, in her widowhood, or take an husband after, shall loose her dower. Fitz. N. B. fo. 144. Regist. fo. 165. V. N. B. fo. 99. V. N. B. fo. 5. See chap. 10. (s), 53. (A).

KING EDWARD THE THIRD,

Borne at Winfor, was crowned, at Weftminfter, the 2. of Feb. 1327, being 15 yeares olde, raigned 50 yeares, 4 months, 24 daies, dyed, the 21. of June, 1377, lyeth buried, in Weftminfter.

Enquiry of Goalers, which shall procure prisoners to become appealers.

(A) STAT. 1. Edw. 3. 7. Be it enacted, for the eschewing the damages, and destruction, that often doth happen by sheriffs, goalers, and keepers of prisons, within franchizes, and without, which have pained their prisoners, and by such evill means, compel, and procure them to become appealers, and to appeal harmless, and guiltless people, to the intent to have ransome of such appealed person, for fear of imprisonment, or other cause, the justices of the one bench, and of the other, and justices of assizes, and goal delivery, shall, by force of this statute, enquire of such compulsive punishments, and procurements, and hear the complaints of all them that will complain, in such cases by bill, and shall hear, and determine such plaints, as well at the suit of the party, as at the kings suit. Stat. 13. Edw. 1. 12. 14. Ed. 3. 10. Raft. pl. fo. 56.

None to ride armed, except, &c.

(B) Stat. 2. Edw. 3. 3. Be it enacted, that none shall ride, or go armed, but such as are the kings servants, or being licenced, nor his officers, to do their office by force of arms, nor bring any force, in an affray of the peace; neither to be armed by day, nor night, in any place, upon pain of forfeiture of their arms, and imprisonment, during the pleasure of the king: All officers whatever is required to put this act in force. See chap. 37. (A).

EDWARD III.

(c) 2. Edw. 3. 6. 2. Edw. 4. 5. Every juftice of peace, upon his difcretion, may bind to the peace, or good behaviour, fuch as are common barrators. A common barrator is he, which is either a common moover, and ftirrer up, or maintainer of fuits in law, in any courts of record, or elfe of quarrels, or parts in the country; as if any court of record, county court, hundred, or other inferior courts, any perfon, by fraud, and malice, under colour of law, fhall themfelves maintain, or ftir up others unto multiplicity of unjuft, and feigned fuits, or informations, upon penal laws, or fhall malicioufly purchafe a fpecial fupplicavit of the peace, to force the other party to yeeld to him compofition, all fuch as are barrators in the countrey, and thefe are three forts.

Firft, difturbers of the peace;* fuch are either common quarrellers, or fighters in their own caufe, or common moovers, or maintainers of quarrels, and affraies between others.

Secondly, common takers, or detainers by force, or fubtlety of the poffeffions of houfes, lands, or goods, which have been in queftion, or controverfie.

Thirdly, inventers, and fowers of falfe reports, whereby difcords arifeth, or may arife between neighbors; yea, if one be *communis feminator litium*, he is a barrator, or if any man, of himfelf, be *communis oppreſor vicinorum*, a common oppreffor of, or wrangler with his neighbors, either by unjuft, or wrangling fuits, or other oppreffions, or deceits, he is a barrator, or if one *communis pacis perturbater, calumniator, et malefaƈtor*, he is a barrator, but all fuch perfons muft be common barrators, not in one, or two, but in many caufes. See Lamb. 79. Co. 8. 36. Co. l. 338. Co. 8. 36. Cromp. 257. Co. 8. 7.

(D) Stat. 2. Edw. 3. 8. It is accorded, and eftablifhed, that it fhall not be commanded by the great feal, nor the little feal, to difturb, or delay common right, and though fuch commandements do come, the This will break the neck of all charters in England, that be unjuft, &c.

the juftices fhall not therefore leave to do right, in any point. Stat. 9. Hen. 3. 29. 5. Ed. 3. 9. 14. Edw. 3. 14.

Gold and filver prohibited, &c.

(E) Stat 9. Edw. 3. 1. No perfon fhall carry gold, or filver out of the realm, without the kings licence; who fo doth, fhall forfeit all fuch as is carrying, with fhip, &c. Stat. 5. Rich. 2. 2. Stat. 2. Hen. 6. 6. 19. Hen. 7. 5.

Rates on victuals.

(F) Stat. 23. Edw. 3. 6. The king ordains, all perfons whatever, which fells any kind of victuals, fhall be bound to fell their victual, at a reafonable rate, or price, having refpect to the price, that fuch victuall be fold at, in the places adjoyning, fo that the feller may have a moderate gain, and not exceffive,* and if the feller do fell otherwife, fhall pay double back. The mayor, and bayliffs of the city, market-towns, and other corporate towns, and the ports of the fea, fhall have power to enquire of all offenders in the fame, and to levy the faid pain (upon themfelves) for their ufe, who fueth for the fame; and in cafe the mayor, and bayliffs, be negligent in putting in execution, any of the premifes, and thereof be convicted, before juftices affigned, then the faid mayor, and bayliffs, fhall be compelled by the faid juftices, to pay the treble of the things fo fold, to the party damnified, and alfo, fhall be grievoufly punifhed by the king. 23. Edw. 3. 4. See chap. 50. (A), 44. (E), 48. (A), 51. (A), 29. (A)..

None to be condemned without his anfwer, &c.

(G) Stat. 28. Edw. 3. 3. The king ordains, that no man, of what eftate, or condition he be, fhall be put

PENALTIES ON MAYORS, SHRIFFS, &c.

put out of his land, nor tenements, nor taken, nor imprifoned, nor dif-inherited, nor put to death, without being brought to anfwer, by due procefs of law. Stat. 9. Hen. 3. 29. 5. Edw. 3. 9. 25. Ed. 3. 4. See chap. 10 (x), 38. (c), 41. (a), 43. (d), 38. (a).

Penalty of a mayor, fheriff, and aldermen, for not redreffing grievances.

(H) Stat. 28. Edw. 3. 10. Becaufe of the errors, defaults, and mifprifions, which be notorioufly ufed in cities, boroughs, and corporations, for default of good governance, of the mayor, fheriff, and aldermen, cannot be inquired, nor found, by people of the fame town, it is ordained, and eftablifhed, that the faid mayor, fheriffs, and aldermen, which have the governance of the faid town, or city, fhall caufe to be redreffed, and corrected, the defaults, errors, and mifprifions above named, and the fame duly punifh, from time to time, upon a certain pain, that is to fay, at the firft default, a thoufand marks to the king, the fecond default, two thoufand marks, and at the third default, that the franchizes, and liberties of the faid town, be taken into the kings hand; it fhall be enquired of by foraign inquefts, of foraign counties, namely, the city of London, but all other cities, boroughs, and corporations, to be tryed by forain inquefts, in the fame town, which may be done by the punifhment of judges, thereunto affigned by inqueft, or indictment, and called to anfwer the fame, out of their town, which fine is to be leavyed by attachment, and diftrefs, and by exigent, if need be, upon any land, or tenements out of their town, belonging to any of them.

KING

KING EDWARD THE SIXTH,

Borne at Hamton Court, at the age of 9 yeares, began his raigne the 31. *of January,* 1546, *crowned, at Weſtminſter the* 20. *of February following. He raigned* 6 *yeares,* 5 *monthes, died, the* 6. *of Julie, buried, at Weſtminſter.*

Murder, &c.

(A) STAT. 1. Edw. 6. 12. It is murder to ſtrike with either blunt, or ſharp weapon, if the party dye within a year and a day, and the blows given upon malice; neither ſhall clergy be allowed. See chap. 36. (A).

Victuallers, and handicrafts-men.

(B) Stat. 2. Edw. 6. 15. For as much as artificers, handicrafts-men, and labourers have made confederacies, and mutually ſworn, not onely that they ſhould ſell their victuals, at a certain rate, and not to meddle with one anothers work, and finiſh that which others have begun, but alſo, to appoint how much work they ſhall do in the day, and what hours, and times they ſhall work, contrary to the laws, and ſtatutes of this realm, and to the hurt, and great impoveriſhment of the kings ſubjects; for reformation whereof, the king ordains, that if any victuallers, or artificers aforeſaid, ſhall at any time combine, conſpire, or make any oaths, that they ſhall not ſell their victuals, at certain prices, or that artificers ſhall not work, but as aboveſaid, being convicted, ſhall pay, in ſix dayes, ten pounds to the king, or twenty dayes impriſonment, and fed onely with bread and water, if he have not ſufficient to pay the ſaid fine; for the ſecond offence, the pillory, or twenty pound, and for the third offence, ſhall

forfeit

EDWARD VI.

forfeit. forty pounds, or elfe be fet in the pillory, and lofe one of his ears, and fhall be taken as an infamous man, and his fayings, and oath, not to be credited in matter of judgement; and if any fuch confpiracy, covenant, or promife be had, or made by any fociety, brotherhood, or company of craft-myftery, or occupation of the myfteries afore-mentioned, with the prefence, or confent of the moſt of them, that then, immediately upon fuch act of confpiracy, covenant, or promife, had, or made, over and befides the particular punifhment, before in this act appointed, for the offender, their corporation fhall be diſſolved, to all intents, conftructions, and purpofes; and that none do prefume to hinder any free-mafon, rough-mafon, carpenter, bricklayer, plafterer, joyner, hard-hewer, fawer, tyler, pavier, glafier, lyme-burner, brick-maker, tyle-maker, plummer, or labourer, born in this realm, or made denifon, to work in the faid crafts, in any city, borough, or town corporate, with any perfon, or perfons that will retain him, albeit the faid perfons, fo retained, or any of them, do not inhabit, or live in the faid town, &c. nor be free of the fame city, &c. any ftatute, law, ordinance, or other thing to the contrary, upon forfeiture of five pound a time, half to the king, and half to the party fuing, to be recovered by bill, &c. No wager of law, or protection, allowed, &c. See chap. 29. (E), 30. (F), 36. (A).

Robbing within a market of a fair, booth, tent, &c.

(c) Stat. 5. 6. Ed. 6. 14. Be it enacted, that no perfon, or perfons which fhall happen to be found guilty, after the laws of this realm, of, and for robbing any perfon, or perfons, in any booth, or tent, in any fair, or market, the owner, his wife, children, or fervant, then being within the fame booth, or tent, fhall not be admitted the benefit of his, or their clergy, but excluded thereof, and fuffer

death,

death, without confideration, whether the faid perfons within, fhall be fleeping, or waking. See chap. 47. (B), 49. (D), 51. (A), 11. (N).

Fore-ftalling, regrators, ingrocers.

(D) Stat. 5. 6. Edw. 6. 14. The law being fo good againft thefe offenders, that I fhall give Poultons expofition thereof, viz. They deferve to be reckoned amongft the number of oppreffors of the common good, and publick weal of the nation, for they do endeavour to enrich themfelves, by the impoverifhing of others, and refpect not how many lofes, fo they may gain.

They have been exclaimed of, and condemned in parliament, from one generation to another, as appears by many ftatutes, at leaft fourteen ftatutes, efpecially fore-ftallers, as appears by 34 Ed. 1. when it was ordained, that no foreftaller, fhould be fuffered to dwell in any town, 'for he is a manifeft oppreffor of the poor, and deceiver of the rich, a publick enemy of the country, a canker, a moth, and a gnawing worm, that daily wafteth the commonwealth. And the name, and act of a foreftaller was fo odious, that it was moved in parliament, to enact, that a foreftaller fhould be bated out of the town, where he dwelt, by dogs, and whipped forth with whips, (Newcaftle would have been empty) and by this ftatute, it declareth who are offenders, and what punifhment to be inflicted.

That whatfoever perfon, or perfons, fhall buy, or caufe to be bought, any merchandize, victual, or other thing, coming by land, or water, towards any fair, or market, to be fold in the fame, or coming towards any city, port, or haven, creek, or road of this nation, from any part, beyond the feas to be fold.

Or make any bargain, contract, or promife for the having, or buying of the fame, or any part of the

the fame, fo coming as aforefaid, before the fame merchandize, victual, or other things fhall be in the market, fair, city, port, haven, creek, or road, ready to be fold ; or fhall make any motion by word, letter, meffage, or otherwife, to any perfon, or perfons, for the inhaufing of the price, or dear felling of any of the other things abovementioned; or elfe diffwade, move, or ftir any perfon coming to the market, or fair, to forbear to bring any of the things above-mentioned, to any fair, or market, city, port, &c. to be fold as aforefaid, fhall be adjudged a foreftaller, 13. Eliz. excepts oyls, fugars, fpices, currans, or other foreign victuals, brought from beyond the fea, fifh, and falt only, excepted.

A regrator, defined. What perfon, or perfons fhall by any means regrate, obtain, or get, into his, or their hands, or poffeffions, in any fair, or market within this nation, to be fold, any dead victual whatfoever brought thither for that purpofe, and do fell the fame again, in any fair, or market holden, or kept in the fame places, or within any market, or fair, within four miles thereof, fhall be reputed, and taken for a regrator, or regrators.

An engroffer, is he, or they which fhall engroffe, or get, into his, or their hands, by buying, con-tracting by promife, taking other then by demife, grant, or leafe of land, or tythe, any corn, growing in the fields, or any other corn, or grain, butter, cheefe, fifh, or other dead victuals whatfoever, within the nation, to the intent to fell the fame again, fhall be reputed, and taken, an unlawful engroffer, or en-groffers.

If any perfon, or perfons fhall offend, in any of the things before recited, and being thereof duly convicted, or attainted thereof, by the laws of this nation, for the firft offence, fhall fuffer two months imprifonment, without bayl, or mainprize, and for-feit the value of the goods, for the fecond offence, fix months imprifonment, without bayl, or main-prize,

prize, and lose double the value of the goods, and upon conviction of the third offence, shall be set in the pillory, where he dwells, in the same town, and lose all the goods, he, or they have, which was to their own use, and be committed to prison, during the kings pleasure. It is but *Mutatis, mutandis.*

Every justices of every county, is to enquire, and determine of the offences, in their quarter-sessions, upon inquisition, presentment, bill, or information, exhibited, and proved by two witnesses, the one half of the fine to the king, the other to the party discoverer.

What justice can be expected, or had in Newcastle, the mayors, justices, and burgesses, being the offenders, judges, (P) jurors in their own causes, and must be tryed in the same county, (T) themselves to have the fines, as by charter appears. * See stat. 21. k. James, 4. (T). See 10. chap. (I.). (P), chap. 10. (R). (*) See stat. 5. Eliz. 12.

The town of Gates-head, and all liberties, given to Newcastle, &c.

(E) Stat. 7. Edw. 6. 10. There being *no* bishop of Durham, elected, nor any member of parliament, for that county, which the mayor, and burgesses of Newcastle, perceiving, petitioned the king, that the town of Gateshead, in the county of Durham, adjoyning to their corporation, only the river of Tyne between, being populous, and without government, and often committing many outrages, in their town, and then got over the water, into the town of Gates-head unpunished, and that often they cast rubbish into the river, and also, that the bridge went to decay very much, which belonged to that town, humbly beseeching, that his majesty, would be graciously pleased, to incorporate that town, with them, under their government, with all its members, and salt-meadows, and park, and that it may be quite

taken

RICHARD II.

taken from the county of Durham, and all the people therein, to become fubordinate to their laws. Be it enacted, that the whole town of Gates-head, with the falt-meadows, the whole water, and bridge, with all the liberties thereunto belonging, except the common, which fhall ftill remain to the inhabitants, be incorporated with Newcaftle, and disjoyned from the county of Durham, as Newcaftle was from Northumberland, by charter.

KING RICHARD THE SECOND,

Borne at Bourdeaux, fonne to Edward, prince of Wales, begann his raigne, the 21. of June, anno. Dom. 1377. He raigned 22 years, was depofed, and died, the 14. of Feb. 1399. Firft, buried at Langley, in Hartfordfhire, and afterwards, at Weftminfter.

A free trade in all England.

(A) STAT. 11. Rich. 2. 7. and the 14. Rich. 2. 9. Be it enacted, that all merchants, aliens, and denifons, and all other, and every of them, of what eftate, or condition they be, which will buy, or fell corn, wine averdepoize, flefh, fifh, and all other victual, or other merchandizes, and all other things vendible, from whencefoever they come, in whatfoever place they pleafe, be it city, borough, town, port, of the fea, fair, market, or other place within this realm, within franchizes, or without, may freely, or without difturbance, fell the fame to whom they pleafe, as well to foreigners, as to denizons, except to the enemies of the king, and of his realm.

And

And if any disturbance be done, to any such merchant, &c. upon his fail of the same, in any of the places aforesaid, the mayor, and bayliffs of such franchizes, shall make remedy, but if they do not, and being thereof convicted, the franchizes shall be taken, into the kings hand, and the party grieving, shall make to the merchant grieved, double damages.

And if such disturbance be out of the franchized towns, then the steward, or bayliffe of such lord, who is lord of the mannor, shall give right, or pay double damages; the party offending shall be imprisoned, for one whole year, and that none such shall be disturbed, but shall freely buy, and sell, for his own use, or to the kings, &c. except that the merchant, aliens, shall carry no wines out of the realm, as it is contained, in their charters.

And that the said things be holden, kept, and performed, in every city, borough, town, port of the sea, or any other place, notwithstanding any charter of franchize, to them granted, to the contrary, nor usage, custome, nor judgement, given upon their charters, usages, nor customes, which they may alleage, which charters, usages, and customes, the said king, the grand-fathers, the prelates, earls, barons, and great men, and commons in parliament aforesaid, holds these said charters, &c. of no force, and as being things, granted, used, and accustomed to the damage of the king, the prelates, earls, barons, and great men of his realm, and great oppression of the commons, saving to the king, and to other, the customes due of the said merchandizes.

And the chancellor, treasurer, and justices, assigned to hold the pleas of the king, in places where they come, shall enquire of such disturbances, and grievances, and do punishment, according as is before ordained.

And

And by a statute, made the 25. Edw. 3. 2. it was ordained, and established, that the said statutes, made in the ninth year, chapter 1. in all points, and articles, contained in the same, should be holden, kept, and maintained, &c.

And if any charter, letters pattents, proclamations, or commandements, usage, allowance, or judgement were made to the contrary, the same should be utterly repealed, avoyded, and holden for none.

And that it is free for any whatever, that brings any provisions whatever, to sell the same, or other merchandizes, by grosse, or retail, either in the city of London, or any other port, city, borough, or town-corporate in England, without challenge, or impeachment, and to sell them freely, to any that will buy the same, notwithstanding any grant whatever, to the contrary, notwithstanding any franchize, custome used, since such franchizes, and customes, usages, be in common prejudice to the king, and all people, &c.

And that no mayor, bayliff, catch-pole, minister, nor other, shall meddle in the sail of any manner of victuals vendible, brought to the places aforesaid.

And all men that will sue, may have a writ out of the chancery, to attach him by his body, that offends herein, as a disturber of the common profit, &c.

The king seeing cleerly if the said statutes were duly put in execution, would much extend to the profits, and wealth of the whole nation, do ordain, and establish, by assent of the prelates, dukes, earls, barons, great men, nobles, and commons, in this present parliament, assembled, that the said statutes, shall be firmly holden, kept, maintained, and fully executed, in all points, and articles of the same, notwithstanding any ordinance, statute, charter, letters pattents, franchizes, proclamations, commandements, usage, allowance, or judgement be made,

or

or ufed to the contrary, it fhall be utterly repealed, avoyded, and holden for none.

This ftatute was obtained, by a petition (worth reading) from all the nobles, and commons of England, as you may read, in the ninth of Edward the third, chapter the firft, it laying open the great grievance of the whole nation, in parliament, of provifions, and other merchandizes, being engroffed into private hands, and reftraining all others from trading, but themfelves, &c. See chap. 29. (c), 30. (D), 32. (D), 35. (A), 38. (A), 51. (B.C).

This ftatute revived, would make England as happy as Venice, for riches, &c.

Merchant-ftrangers fhall be well ufed.

(B). Stat. 14. Rich. 2. 9. Be it enacted, that merchant-ftrangers, repairing into the realm of England, fhall be well, and courteoufly, and rightfully intreated, and governed in the faid realm, to the intent, that they fhall have the courage to repair into the fame. See chap. 30. (B), 41. (A).

The duke of Venice, by tollerating a free trade, all the nobility, and gentry trades in merchandizings, which doth fo improve his revenew, that it maintains his wars, without other impofitions, he being able to wage war with the moft potenteft prince that is, &c.

No cuftomers to be traders, nor to have parts of fhips.

(c) Stat. 14. Rich. 2. 10. The king ordains, that no cuftomers, nor controlers have any fhips of their own, nor meddle with the fraught of fhips, and to efchew as well the damage of the king, of his cuftoms, as the loffe of the merchants, repairing to the port, as well aliens, as denizons; and that no cuftomer, controler, fearcher, waiter, or finder, have any fuch office for terme of life, but onely,

as

as long as shall please the king, notwithstanding any pattent, or grant to any, to the contrary, but such pattents, or grants, be repealed, and of no force, nor value. Stat. 17. Rich. 2. See chap. (35).

Statute of mortmain.

(D) Stat. 15. Rich. 2. 5. Be it enacted, what mayors, bayliffs, and commons of cities, boroughs, and other towns, which have perpetual commonalty, and others, which have officers, that from henceforth, they shall not purchase to them, and their commons, any lands, &c. nor no religious, or other person, whatever he be,* do buy, or sell, or under colour of gift, or terme, or any other manner of title, any lands, tenements, upon pain of forfeiture of the same, whereby the said lands, and tenements, might have come to mortmain.

Riots, routs, &c.

(E) The 4. year, king Rich. 2. Riots, routs, and unlawfull assemblies, have been so many times pernicious, and fatal enemies, to the peace, and tranquility of the nation, that it did shake the foundation, and form of state-government, as that of a collector of a subsidy, at Dartford, in Kent, in his days, in requiring but a groat of a taylor, and his wife, grew to such a head of discontentment, and not being timely queld, became such a rebellion, that it put the king in great hazard of his life, the burning of the city of London, the nobles, and gentry, with the learned of the law, beheaded, and others, in hazard of their lives, and families overthrown, and the records of law burnt. Wat. Tyler was captain. See Hen. 6. (D). See chap. 37. (A).

A 2   QUEEN

QUEEN MARY.

Maria, nata Grenouici, 11. *Febru.* 1505, *infipit, regnare,* 6. *Juli,* 1553. *Regnavit,* 5 *annos, et* 4 *menfis, obyt, annos nata,* 45, *et* 9 *menfis.*

The town of Gates-head taken from Newcaftle.

(A) STAT. 1. Mary, chap. 3. So foon as bifhop Tunftall was created bifhop of Durham, laid open to the queen, and parliament, the illegallity of Gates-heads being taken from the county of Durham, and incorporated with Newcaftle, and how furreptitioufly they got it paft, by act of parliament, and humbly befeeched, that the town, and liberties of Gates-head, might be reftored to the county of Durham again, which could not well be done, without that ftatute of the 7. Edw. 6. 10. were repealed. After a great debate in parliament, it was found onely a covetous difpofition, in the corporation of Newcaftle, to require that from king Edward the fixth, and in no wayes for the good of any, in any particular fenfe, who enacted, that the ftatute of the feventh of Edward the fixth, chapter the tenth, fhould be repealed, and of no force, to all intents, and purpofes, and the town of Gates-head fhould be free, from the corporation of Newcaftle, &c. See chap. 7. and chap. 8.

SWEET QUEEN.

MARY I.

Bloody
ELIZABETH.

QUEEN ELIZABETH.

The most *excellent princes Elizabeth, queene of Englande, France, and Ireland, defendor of the faith, &c. She raigned* 44 *yeares, died, the* 24. *of March,* 1602, *aged* 69, 6 *monthes, and lieth buried, at Westminster.*

How long apprentices should serve.

(A) STAT. 5. Eliz. 4. Be it enacted, that all apprentices, in every corporate town, through England, shall serve, after the custome, and order of London, the full term of seven years, at least, so as the terme, and years of such apprentices, do not expire, or determine, before such apprentices be of the age of four and twenty years, at least; and if an apprentice be mis-used, by the non-conformity of the master, then, the next officer, upon complaint, shall bind the master to answer the sessions, and the cause appearing, the bench may discharge the apprentice from his master. See chap. 55. (c).

The punishment of perjury, &c.

(B) Stat. 5. Eliz. 9. Be it enacted, that if any person, or persons, at any time, shall unlawfully, and corruptly, procure any witnesse, or witnesses, by letters, rewards, or any other promises, to commit any wilful, and corrupt perjury, in any matter, or cause whatsoever, now depending, or which hereafter shall depend, in suit, or variance, by any writ, action, bill, complaint, or information, upon any matter, or cause whatever, and being thereof convicted, shall forfeit forty pound; and if he have not so much, then to be imprisoned for half a yeer, without bail, or mainprize, and to stand in the pillory, one hour, in a market day, in the open market, and never to

A a 2   be

be received as a witnesse, in any courts of record; and if judgement be given, upon his testimony, it shall be void, and the party grieved have his damages.

And if any person shall wilfully perjure himself, by committing wilful perjury, by his deposition in any courts, or being examined, *Ad perpetuam rei memoriam*, for which offence, he shall forfeit twenty pound, and imprisonment for six months, without bail, or mainprize, and never to be as a witnesse in any court, and that the oath shall be void, and party grieved to recover his damages; and if he be not able to pay his fine, then to be set in the pillory, having both his ears nayled thereunto, and never to be credited again in any court; the one half of the fine to the queen, and the other to the party grieved, that will sue for the same, by bill of indictment, &c. wherein there shall be no wager of law, &c.

And all witnesses are required, upon summons, to appear, to give evidence, reasonable charges allowed; and upon default, to forfeit ten pound, and all the damages sustained, to be recovered in any court of record, by action, bill, &c. No wager of law, &c. See stat. 21. k. James, 28. made perpetual. See chap. 31. (A), 34. (A.B), 42. (A).

Fore-stallers of corn, &c.

(c) Stat. 5. Eliz. 12. Be it enacted, that no person, or persons, shall buy any corn, out of open fair, or market, to sell again, unlesse such persons shall have special, and expres words in a licence, that he, or they, may so do, upon pain of the forfeiture of five pounds, for so doing, which forfeiture to come to the queen, the one half, and the other half to the party that will sue for the same, by bill, &c. See stat. 5. 6. Ed. 6. 14. See chap. 50. (A), 51. (C).

Arrestings

Arreſtings in other mens names, and delays, &c.

(D) Stat. 8. Eliz. 2. Be it enacted, by this preſent parliament, that if any perſon, or perſons, ſhall by any means cauſe, or procure, any other perſon to be arreſted, or attached, at the ſuit, or in the name of any perſon, where indeed no ſuch perſon is known, or without the aſſent, conſent, or agreement of ſuch perſons, at whoſe ſuit, or in whoſe name, ſuch arreſt, or attachment is, or ſhall be ſo had, and procured, that then, every ſuch perſon, and perſons, that ſhall ſo cauſe, or procure any ſuch arreſt, or attachment of any other perſon, to be had, or made for vexation, or trouble, and ſhall thereof be convicted, or lawfully accuſed, by indictment, preſentment, or by the teſtimony of two ſufficient witneſſes, or more, or other due proof, ſhall, for every ſuch offence, by him, or them committed, done, or procured, have, and ſuffer impriſonment of his, or their body, ſix months, without bail, or mainprize, and before a deliverance out of priſon, ſhall pay unto the party, ſo arreſted, or attached, treble the coſts, and charges, damages, and expences, that he, or they ſhall be put unto, by reaſon, or occaſion of ſuch arreſt, or attachment ſo had, and ſhall alſo forfeit, and pay unto ſuch perſon, or perſons, in whoſe name, or at whoſe ſuit, he, or they, ſhall ſo procure ſuch arreſt, or attachment to be had, or made, if then there be any ſuch perſon known, the ſumme of ten pounds, for every ſuch offence; and that all ſuch perſons, damnified thereby, ſhall have their remedy in any court of record, by bill, plaint, or action of debt, for all damages, &c. wherein there ſhall not be any eſſoyn, protection, or wager of law, allowed the defendant. See ſtat. 13. Ed. 1. 36.

The

The penalty of cutting of purses.

(E) Stat. 8. Eliz. 4. Whereas there are a certain people, of a fraternity, or brother-hood, that puts in practice that art, or myftery, of cutting of purfes, and that do combine fecretly, to fpoyl the true fubjects of this realm, be it therefore enacted, that whofoever be found guilty of taking away monies, &c. in fuch fort, from any perfon, or perfons, fhall not have the benefit of clergy. See chap. 12. (5), 39. (A).

Sheriffs fees for executing executions, &c.

(F) Stat. 29. Eliz. 4. Be it enacted by, this prefent parliament, that it fhall not be lawful for any fheriff, or bayliff of franchizes, or liberties, or any of the officers, or deputies, nor any of them, by colour, or reafon of their, or either of their office, or offices, to have, receive, or take of any perfon whatever, directly, or indirectly, for the ferving, and executing of any extent, or execution, upon the body, lands, goods, or chattels of any perfon, or perfons whatfoever, more, or other confideration, or recompence, than as in this prefent act fhall be limited, and appointed, which fhall be lawful to be had, received, and taken, that is to fay, twelve pence, of, and for every twenty fhillings, where the fumme exceedeth not one hundred pounds, and fix pence, of, and for every twenty fhillings, being over and above the faid fumme of one hundred pounds, that he, or they fhall levie, or extend, and deliver in execution, or take the bodie in execution for, by vertue, and force of fuch extent, or execution whatfoever, upon pain, and penalty, that all, and every fheriff, &c. that do the contrary, fhall lofe, and forfeit to the party grieved, his treble damages, and fhall forfeit forty pound, for every time fo offending, the half thereof to the queen, and the other to the party fuing, by bill, plaint, action, or information, wherein no effoyn, wager,

wager of law, or protection, fhall be allowed. This ftatute not to extend to any city, or town corporate.

The poor to be fet on work.

(G) Stat. 43. Eliz. 2. Be it enacted, by this prefent parliament, and the authority thereof, that all poor be fet on work, by the church-wardens, or overfeers, and fuch as will not work, being able, fhall be fent to the houfe of correction. See chap. 38. (A.C).

Sheriffes punifhable for falfe arrefts, &c.

(H) Stat. 43. Eliz. 6. For the avoyding many fuits commenced, according to the due courfe of the laws of this realm, to the intollerable vexation, and charge of her highneffe fubjects, be it enacted, by authority of this parliament, if any fheriff, or other perfon, having authority, or taking upon him to break writs, or make any warrant, for the fummoning of any perfon, upon any writ, proceffe, fuit, or for arreft, or attaching of any perfon, or perfons, by his, or their body, or goods, to appear in any of her majefties courts, at Weftminfter, or elfewhere, not having before, that originall writ, or proceffes, warranting the fame, that then, upon complaint made to the juftices of affize, of the county, where the fame offence fhall be committed, or to the judges of the court, out of which the procefs iffued, not only the party that made fuch warrant, but all thofe that were the procurers thereof, fhall be fent for, before the faid judges, or juftices, by attachment, or otherwife, as the fame judges, or juftices, fhall think good, and allow of, and be examined thereof, upon their oaths; and if the fame offence be confeffed, by the fame offenders, or proved, by fufficient witneffes, to the fatisfaction of the fame judges, or juftices, that then the fame judges, or juftices, justices, that shall so examine the same, shall forthwith, by force of this act, commit every of the same to the gaole, and there shall remain, without bayl, or mainprize, untill such time as they, amongst them, have fully satisfied, and paid unto the party grieved, by such warrant, not onely the summe of ten pounds, but also all costs, and damages, as the same judges, or justices shall set down, that the same party hath sustained thereby, and withall, twenty pound a peece, for their offence to her majesty. 21. king James, chap. 16. 3. king Charles, chap. 4. Dyer, fo. 244.

KING JAMES.

(A) UPON the seventh day of May, in the first year of k. James, a proclamation was proclaimed, throughout London, for to cease all exactions, all monopolies, and all protections whatever, that was against the common good, and that hindered mens suits at law, also forbidding oppression.

Stabbing or thrusting.

(B) Stat. 1. king James, 8. It is enacted, that if any person, or persons, shall stab, or thrust any person, or persons, that hath not then any weapon drawn, or that hath not then first stricken the party, which shall so stab, or thrust, so as the person, or persons, so stabbed, or thrust, shall thereof dye, within the space of six months, then next following, although it cannot be proved that the same was done of malice fore-thought, yet the party, so offending, and being thereof convict, by the verdict of twelve men, confession, or otherwise, according to the laws
of

of this realm, fhall be excluded from the benefit of his, or their clergy, and fhall fuffer death, as in cafe of wilfull murder. Stat. Homicide (24).

Attornies abufes remedied, &c.

(c) Stat. 3. king James, chap. 7. Be it enacted, for redreffe of fundry abufes, committed by attornies, and folicitors, by charging their clients with exceffive fees, and other unneceffary demands, to the great prejudice of the ferjeant, and councellor at law, who is greatly flandered, and to work the private gain of fuch attornies, and folicitors, the client is often extraordinarily delayed, be it enacted, that for the future, that no attorney, folicitor, or fervant to any, fhall be allowed from his clyent, or mafter, of, or for any fee, given to any ferjeant, or councellor at law, or of, or for any fumme, or fummes of mony given for copies, to any clerk, or clerks, or officers, in any court of record, at Weftminfter, unleffe he have a ticket fubfcribed, with the hand, and name of the fame ferjeant, councellor, clerk, or clerks, or officers aforefaid, teftifying how much he hath received for his fee, or paid, or given for copies, and at what time, and how often; and that all attornies, and folicitors, fhall give a true bill unto their mafters, or clyents, or their affigns, of all other charges concerning their fuits, which they have for them, fubfcribed with their own hand, and name, before fuch time, as they, or any of them fhall charge their clyents, with any of the fame fees, or charges; and that if any attorney, or folicitor do, or fhall willingly delay his clyents fuits, to work his own gain, or demand, by his bill, any other fumme of mony, or allowance, upon his account, of any monies which he hath not laid out, or difburfed, that in every fuch cafe the party grieved fhall have his action, againft fuch attorney, or folicitor, and fhall recover therein cofts, and treble damage, and the said attorney, or solicitor, shall be discharged from thenceforth, from being an attorney, or solicitor any more. See chap. 58. (A).

All monopolies, and dispensations, with penal laws, shall be void.

(D) Stat. 21. k. James, chap. 3. For as much as your most excellent majestie, in your royal judgement, and of your blessed disposition, to the weal, and quiet of your subjects, did, in the year of our Lord God, 1610, publish in print, to the whole realm, and to all posterity, that all grants, and monopolies, and of the benefit of any penal laws, or of power to dispense with the law, or to compound for the forfeiture, are contrary to your majesties laws, with your majesties declaration, which is truly consonant, and agreeable, to the ancient, and fundamental laws of this your realm; and whereas your majesty was further gratiously pleased, expresly to command, that no suitor should presume to move your majestie, for matters of that nature, yet neverthelesse upon mis-information, and untrue pretences of publick good, many such grants have been unduly obtained, and unlawfully put in execution, to the great grievance, and inconvenience of your majesties subjects, contrary to the laws, of this your realm, and contrary to your majesties royal, and blessed intention, so published as aforesaid; for avoiding whereof, and preventing the like, for the time to come, may it please your most excellent majestie, at the humble suit of the lords spiritual, and temporal, and the commons, in this present parliament assembled, that it may be declared, and enacted, and be it declared, and enacted, by authority of this present parliament, that all monopolies, and all commissions, grants, licences, charters, and letters pattents heretofore made, or granted to any person, or persons, bodies politick, or corporate, whatsoever, whatfoever, of, or for the fole buying, felling, making, working, or ufing of any thing, within this realm, or of any other monopolies, or of power, liberty, or faculty, to difpence with any other, to give licence, or toleration to do, ufe, or exercife any thing againft the tenure, or purport of any law, or ftatute, or to give, or make any warrant, for any fuch difpenfation, licence, or toleration to be had, or made, &c. and all proclamations, inhibitions, reftraints, warrants of affiftance, and all other matters, or things whatfoever, any way tending to the inftituting, erecting, ftrengthning, furthering, or countenancing of the fame, or any of them, are contrary to the laws of this realm, and fo are, and fhall be utterly void, and of none effect, and in no wayes to be put in ufe or execution, &c.

Be it further enacted, &c. that all perfon, and perfons, bodies politick, and corporate whatfoever, which now are, or hereafter fhall be, fhall ftand, and be dif-abled, and uncapable to have, ufe, exercife, or put in eure, any monopoly, or any fuch commiffion, grant, licence, charter, letters pattents, proclamations, inhibition, reftraint, warrant of affiftance, or other matter, or thing, tending as aforefaid, or any liberty, power, or faculty grounded, or pretended to be grounded, upon them, or any of them.

The party grieved, by pretext of any monopoly, &c. fhall recover his, or their treble damages, and double cofts, &c. and he that delayeth an action, grounded upon ftatute, incurs a premunire, which is expreft in the 16. Rich. 2. 5. fhall be put out of the kings protection, and their lands, and tenements, goods, and chattles, forfeit to our lord the king, and their bodies to be attached, to anfwer the king, &c. (Charters, granted to corporations, faved). (Letters pattents, to ufe new manufactures faved). (Grants, confirmed by acts of parliament, faved). (Warrants, granted to juftices, faved). (Letters pattents, that concern printing, falt-peter, gun-powder, great ordnance shot, or offices, saved). Nor shall this statute extend, to void commissions, for allum mines, nor to the licenses of keeping taverns, making glasse, transportation of calves skins, nor for making smalt, nor for melting iron evre, with sea-coal, &c. provided also, and be it enacted, that this act, or any declaration, proviso, penalty, forfeiture, or other thing before mentioned, shall not extend, or be prejudicial to any use, custome, prescription, franchize, freedome, jurisdiction, immunity, liberty, or priviledge, heretofore claimed, used, or enjoyed, by the governours, and stewards, and brethren of the fellowship of the hoast-men, of the town of Newcastle upon Tyne, or by the ancient fellowship, guild, or fraternity, commonly called hoast-men, for, or concerning the selling, carrying, lading, disposing, shipping, venting, or trading of, or for any sea-coals, stone-coals, or pit-coals, forth, or out of the haven, and river of Tyne, or to a grant, made by the said governor, and stewards, and brethren of the fellowship of the said hoastmen, to the late queen Elizabeth,* of any duty, or summes of money, to be paid for, or in respect of any such coals, as aforesaid. Here the reader may see, that all these excepted, except to the justices, are allowed to be monopolies, and this last, the greatest that ever was. See chap. 11. chap. 8. (A), chap. 21. (A), parliament 1640.

*This is the grant of 1s. per chaldron, that they make the nation pay, &c.

Informations upon penal statutes shall be prosecuted, in the counties, where the offences are committed.

(E) Stat. 21. k. James, chap. 3. Be it enacted, that all informations, upon penal statutes, shall be prosecuted, in the counties, where the offences were committed, &c. upon default of proving that the offence was committed, in the same county, the defendant shall be found not guilty, &c. the informer shall make oath, that the offence was committed, in the same county, where the suit is commenced, &c.
The

The defendant, in an information, upon a penal statute, may plead the general issue, that they are not guilty, &c. Certain offences there be excepted, but may be tried elsewhere, &c.

This statute was made in favour, and ease of the people from coming to London, but it is the worst statute that ever was made, and much in favour of the offender, for the offender, in corporations, and sheriffs, are judges, and jurors, in their own cases, and the informer cast into prison, when the judges are coming to assizes, &c. so the judges cannot come to the knowledge of such offences, and the offenders not punished.

If that clause of the statute were repealed, which tyes all informations to be tryed only, and to be prosecuted in the same county, and this put in, that any may as well profecute at Westminster, as elsewhere, would bring into the publick revenew, above a hundred thousand pound per annum.

Limitations of certain actions, for avoiding suits in law.

(F) Stat. 21. k. James, chap. 16. Be it enacted, that all actions upon the case (other then for flander) actions for account, actions for trespass, debt, detriment, and replevi for goods, or chattel, and the said action of trespass, *quare claufum fregit*, within six years next, after the cause of such action, and not after.

Action of trespass, of assault, battery, wounding, imprisonment, or any of them, within four years next, after the cause of such action, or suit, and not after.

And actions upon the case, for words, within two years next, after the words spoken, and not after.

That no person do enter into any lands, but within twenty years next, after his right, or title, which shall hereafter first descend, or accrue to the same, and in default thereof, such persons, so not
entring

entring, and their heirs, fhall be utterly excluded, and dif-abled, from fuch entry, after to be made &c.

Provided, that if any perfon, or perfons, be at the time of fuch caufe of action, given, or accrued, fallen, or come within the age of one and twenty yeers, *feme covert, non compos mentis,* imprifoned, or be beyond the feas, that then fuch perfon, or perfons, fhall be at liberty to bring the fame actions, fo as they take the fame within fuch time, as are before limited, after their coming to, or being of full age, difcovert, of found memory, at large, and returned from beyond the fea, as other perfons, having no fuch impediments, fhould be done. Stat. 20. Hen. 3. 8. 3. Ed. 1. 38. 32. Hen. 8. 2. 1. M. 5.

The punifhment of drunkards.

(o) Stat. 21. k. James, 7. &c. For preventing of that loathfome fin of drunkenneffe, enacted, that for every time any was drunk, fhould, within one week, after conviction, by the oath of one witneffe, pay five fhillings to the church-wardens of the parifh, for the ufe of the poor, and for want thereof in monies, to be fet in the ftocks fix hours; and for the fecond offence, to be bound to the good behaviour. (See chap. 55. (B).

The ale-houfe keeper, which doth not fell by a full meafure of a quart, fhall, &c. and that fhall keep any perfon, tipling, above one hour, fhall forfeit ten fhillings; and all brewers that fhall deliver beer, to houfes unlicenced, fhall pay fix fhillings eight pence, for every barrel, &c.

KING

KING CHARLES.

The petition of right.

(A) STAT. 3. year of k. Charles, upon the fecond day of March, 1627. The lords fpiritual, and temporal, and the commons, affembled in parliament, read the petition unto the king, the effect thereof was, that his majefty would declare, and grant, in open parliament, that none might be compelled, to make, or yeeld any gift, loan, or benevolence, tax, or fuch like charge, without common confent, by act of parliament.

That none be compelled to make anfwer, or take fuch oath, or to give attendance, or be confined, molefted, or difquieted, for refufal of that.

Nor free-men be imprifoned, or detained, it being the right, and liberty of the fubject, according to the laws, and ftatutes of England, and to declare your royal will, and pleafure, which the king did, in thefe words, (*Soit droit fait come eft defire*) Let right be done as is defired). See 28. chap. 30. (B), 38. (C), 41. (A), 51. (C), 43. (D).

The ftar-chamber, and high-commiffion courts, voted down.

(B) Act 17. king Charles. The parliament diffolved the high-commiffion, and ftar-chamber courts, with the prefident, and councel of the north, to the end, to abandon all arbitrary preffures, conceiving them to be the greateft of evils. The proceedings, cenfures, and decreafe of thofe courts, have, by experience, been found to be an intolerable burden to the people, and the means to introduce an arbitrary power, and government, being contrary to the laws, and liberties of the land, &c. all which courts, and proceedings, fhall ceafe, after the firft of Auguft,

August, 1641 being, absolutely diffolved, and taken away, &c. Be it further enacted, and declared, that neither his majefty, nor councel have, nor ought to have any jurifdiction, power, or authority, by Englifh bill, petition, articles, libel, or any other arbitrary way whatfoever, to examine, or draw into queftion, determine, or difpofe of the lands, tenements, hereditaments, goods, or chattels, of any of the fubjects of this kingdome, but that the fame ought to be tried, and determined, in the ordinary courts of juftice, and by the ordinary courfe of the law, &c. and that from henceforth, no court, councel, or place of judicature, fhall be erected, ordained, conftituted, or appointed, within this realm of England, &c. which fhall have, ufe, or exercife the fame, or the like* jurifdiction, as is, or hath been ufed, practifed in the faid court of ftar-chamber; and be it enacted, that if any, whoever they be, fhall put in practice, any of the courts above named practices, fhall, for fuch offence, forfeit five hundred pound, for the firft offence, to the party grieved, one thoufand, for the fecond offence, and for the third offence, fhall be from thenceforth incapable, *Ipfo facto*, to bear office, and difabled, to make any gift, grant, conveyance, &c. of any of his lands, &c. nor to have any benefit of them, &c. and fhall pay to the party grieved, treble damages, to be recovered, &c. in any court of record, at Weftminfter, by action of debt, bill, plaint, or information, wherein no effoyn, protection, wager of law, ayd, prayer, priviledge, injunction, or order of reftraint, fhall be in any wife prayed, granted, or allowed, nor any more then one imparlence, &c.

It will do the mafters of fhips no harm, to get five hundred pounds, for every oath they are forced to fwear againft themfelves, to cut purfes, to be imprifoned, without judgement of the law, arbitrarily fined, &c. all being done by the magiftrates of Newcaftle, &c. See chap. 29. chap. 26.

THE

THE PARLIAMENT.

Monopolies voted down, &c.

(A) 1640. The parliament were then so zealous, for the nations weal, that seeing what heavy yokes of bondage the people sat under, by monopolies, they fell to work on them, and voted down the pattents of tyn, soap, leather, salt, &c. as being infringers of the common right of the free-born; and the pre-emption of coals would have been the like, if any publick spirit had appeared, and presented that grand grievance, which more concerns the life of man, then any of the other, but I hope God will do it in due time. See stat. 21. king James 3. See chap. 44. (E).

All trade prohibited to Newcastle upon Tyne, &c.

(B) 9. Jan. 1642. Ordained, that all trade to Newcastle upon Tyne, for coals, salt, &c. be prohibited, upon pain of forfeiture, and confiscation of ship, and goods, by reason that town is conceived to be the principal inlet, of all foreign aid, and forces, for strengthening themselves against the parliament, tending to the destruction of the laws, and liberties of England.

An ordinance for a low price of coals, &c.

(c) Feb. and June, 42. and 43. Two ordinances were made, for setting a rate upon coals, at London; being so scarce, and enhansed to such a great rate, that all the poor were in a very sad condition.

Propositions to reduce Newcastle, &c.

(D) 5. June, 1643. An ordinance for reducing Newcastle, to the obedience of the parliament; being garrisoned

garrisoned, and kept by papists, and other ill-affected persons, whereby the whole land suffers, for want of coals, so absolutely necessary to the maintenance, and support of life, which falls heavy upon the meaner sort.

Upon the 20. of June, the lord mayor, and court of aldermen, and common councel, of the city of London, met at Guild-hall, and undertook the reducing of that town of Newcastle, from their malignancy, upon the propositions of parliament, whereby they were to be repaid, both principle, and use of all charges, out of the gentlemens estates of Northumberland, and county of Durham, (it was *summa injuria*, that these gentlemen should be destroyed, for the offence, and wickednesse of that corporation, who never yet suffered for the same, &c.).

Ordinances of Parliament.

(E) 12. May, 1643. Ordained, that there be a free, and open trade, in the ports of Sunderland, in the county of Durham, and Blithe, in the county of Northumberland, to relieve the poor inhabitants thereabouts by reason of the rapines, and spoyls, those enemies of Newcastle have brought upon them, in those two counties, they all being in great want, and extremity.

(F) 14. Novem. 1644. Ordained, that a free, and open trade be had to Newcastle, for coals, salt, &c. that corporation being won by the sword, with the scots, &c. These are breviated in the epistle to the reader, &c.

Notwithstanding all these sad events, which that corporation brought upon the people, in those northern counties, but the mayor, and burgesses, most of which were the transgressors, not in the least sorry, but still doth, with the highest hand of arrogancy, and pride, tyrannize over the people, in those counties, not admitting them to improve their estates, but

casts

casts them into prison, &c. The oppressed cries for relief, and could never be heard.

(G) 17. June, 1649. An act of parliament passed, for sail of kings lands, and queens, &c. by vertue whereof was surveyed in lands, mils, and tenements, to the value of two thousand pounds per annum, and returned to Worcester house. I leave the rest to the examiner, &c. The particulars, I have, &c.

(H) —— 1650. An act of parliament, constituting a councel, for regulating of trade, throughout England, &c. and were to sit at White-hall, where there was a legal tryal had against Newcastle, and were overthrown, as by the report, which was drawn up, by the said councel, to be reported, to the parliament, as appears, &c.

(I) Anno 1653. The parliament impowred a committee, for regulating of trade, and corporations, through England, &c. when more charge was brought in against the evill practice of the said corporation, appears, &c.

All that is desired, is a free trade in the river of Tyne, according to the purport, and true meaning of that stat. 11. Rich. 2. 7. The taking away what is bad, in that corporations charter, the river preserved, and men from being imprisoned, without judgement of law.

Now to give some reasons against this arbitrary power.

AS Sir Walter Raleigh, being to give a character of Henry the eighth, prefaceth his description, with this introduction, *If all the pictures, and patterns of a merciless prince, were lost in the world, they might all again be painted to the life, out of the story of that king.*

So having given the world an account of the most unchristian, illegal, oppressive practices of the magistrates of Newcastle, upon the people of this nation, whose either neighbourhood, or calling, or condition of life, necessitate them to an intercourse with them, either by way of traffique, or any other way, though forced into that port, and harbor, by distress of weather, tempest, or any other accident, incident to those that go down to the seas in ships, and occupie their businesses in the waters; reflecting on their actions, I may safely say of them, as that noble knight did, of that king, *If all the pictures, and patterns of a cruel, and merciless people, were utterly lost in the world, they might be all painted to the life, out of this narrative,* setting out the illegal oppressions, arbitrary exactions, barbarous murthers practised, and committed, by the magistrates of Newcastle, both on their neighbors, and the free people of this nation.

There are two rules, or canons in scripture, upon which all the commandements of the second table, (and consequently, all the duty of man to his neighbor) do depend.

The first is, *Quod tibi fieri non vis alteri ne feceris, What thou wouldst not have another do unto thee, that thou oughtest not do unto another.* This rule, well observed,

served, prevents all injury, and wrong; for while a man frames his own actions, towards his neighbor, according to that pattern, which, in his own breast, he shapes to his neighbor, to perform unto himself, hee will do no injury, becaufe he would receive no injury; and this is the ground of that command, or precept of our Saviour, *Thou shalt love thy neighbor as thyself*.

The fecond rule is, *Whatfoever yee would that men should do unto you, even do yee unto them*, Mat. 7. 12. and this rule stirs us up to all beneficence, and doing good to our neighbor; for as to prevent injuring another man, a man should afke himself, would I that another man should do to me, as I am about to do unto him? and fo, love to himfelf, will prevent hatred to another; fo to confer favors, and to do good unto another, a man should afke himself, would I require this boon, this favor, this good turn from another, if I ftood in need of it, as my neighbor doth, and I were in his condition? and would the granting, or doing this favor, be moft acceptable to me, and lay an eternal obligation upon me? Hence, love to a mans felf, will kindle his bowels of compaffion to his brother, and will difpofe him willingly to do that good unto another, which, if occafion ferved, he would willingly receive from another.

Thefe men of Newcaftle regulate themfelves, in all their actions here charged upon them, and fully proved, by oath of men, of undoubted integrity, neither by the one rule, nor by the other; for they do not onely do thofe injuries, and wrongs, which they would not take, but they deny thofe favors, which they would, if occafion ferved, willingly receive; nay, they do not onely deny to do thofe favors themfelves, which, not onely, by the law of chriftian charity, but even by the dictate of nature, and common humanity they are bound to perform, but they hinder, and deter thofe that would do them,

and

and violently profecute, fine, and imprifon thofe who have relieved them, and without their prefent help, had fhip-wracked in the very haven, and perifhed, under the expectation of a delayed affiftance.

I fhall not accufe all incorporations, as eftablifhed monopolies, but certainly the corporation of New-caftle, as it is managed by thofe men, is, of all monopolies, the moft oppreffive, and confequently the moft odious monopolie; rendred fo by thofe injurious, deftructive, illegal priviledges, which, againft all law of God, and man, they have made, and indulged to themfelves, and accordingly, are rigoroufly practifed by them. But that their monftrous practices may more clearly appear, to all the world, what hath been fcattered, and divided, by neceffary interweaving of proofs, and depofitions, ftatutes, and laws, and other fupplements, I fhall here contract, into a narrow compafs, and prefent them, *Brevi quafi tabellâ,* unto the view of the world. Their tyranny, and oppreffion, may be reduced to thefe heads.

Marginal note: It would not be amifs for the honeft burgeffes to proteft againft the difhoneft, to the end, the innocent may not fuffer for the nocent; their oath is not to uphold fuch actings.

Firft, *Falfe Imprifonments,* without any tryal of law, or offence committed; (pag. 77. 95. 61. 82. 90. 92. 99. 91. 109. 64. 87. 113. 95) When the chief prieft, and elders of the jews, defired Feftus, on their information, barely to pafs fentence upon St. Paul, (though a heathen judge) he returns them this anfwer, *It is not the manner of the Romans, to deliver any man to die, before that he, which is accufed, have the accufers face to face, and have licence, to anfwer for himfelf,* Act. 25. 16. On the unjuftice, and unreafonablenefs of this courfe, doth Nicodemus oppofe the chief priefts, and pharifees, in the behalf of Chrift, *Doth our law,* (faith he) *judge any man, before it hear him, and know what he hath done,* John 7. 51. (p. 166. G). This way of proceeding, in judicatory, is moft repugnant, both to the law of nature, as you fee in the Romans law, and, alfo, to the law of God, which pofitively determines, *One witnefs*

nefs shall not rise up against a man, for any iniquity, or any sin, that he sinneth; at the mouth of two, or three witnesses, shall the matter be established, Deut. 19. 15. and if God would not have any man, to be condemned, in any judicatory, by the testimony of one witness, but by the joynt attestation of two, or three, at least, as is evident, by this text of scripture, and by many concurrent places of divine writ, as *Numb*. 35. 30. *Deut*. 17. 6. *Mat*. 18. 16. *John*, 8. 17. *Heb*. 10. 28. 2. *Cor*. 13. 1. How much less would God approve of such tyrannical proceedings, to condemn a man, without any witness at all, or ever permitting the person accused, to take up an apology, or just defence for himself.

Secondly, *Forcing men to swear against themselves*, (pag. 64. 78. 92. 93. 94. 97. 98. 109.) How highly were the hearts of this nation inflamed? what indignation did they conceive against the practices both of the star chamber, and high commission, heretofore, (pag. 93.) as laying an unsupportable yoak upon the necks of the people, by the tender of the oath, *ex officio?* Hath all the nation freed themselves from this bondage, by a good law, so that elsewhere no man is compelled to testifie against himself, or where other witnesses fail, inforced to accuse himself? and must they onely, that come under the jurisdiction of the magistrates of Newcastle, remain inflaved under the same bondage? Is this tyranny lawfull at Newcastle, that is exploded, and cast off every where else?

Nay, that which infinitely heightens their oppression, and wickedness, is this, that those reasons which were alledged, to justifie this practice, (pag. 191. 94. 93. 92. 109.) both in the star chamber, and high commission, have no place of pretension here. There the zeal of justice, to let no sin go unpunished, and the glory of God, in the sinners confession, and accusing of himself, as Joshua abjured Achan, *My son, give I pray thee glory to the Lord God of Israel, and*

make

make confeſſion unto him ; and tell me now, what thou haſt done, hide it not from me, Joſh. 7. 19. was alleged as an inſtance, to juſtifie their proceedings, where otherwiſe the offender could not be diſcovered, either by evidence of the fact, or teſtimony of witneſſes; but here, by an oath, they compel men to reveal the ſecrets of their hearts, to riſe up in judgement againſt themſelves, for no other end, but by their own confeſſion, to make them guilty, and then invade their fortunes. Firſt, they make themſelves maſters of their conſciences, (pag. 92. 114. 106.) and by that make themſelves maſters of their eſtates. Covetouſneſs, and not zeal of juſtice, or Gods glory, is the principle from whence they act.

Thirdly, *Impoſing fines arbitrarily*, (p. 25. (F), 34. (R), 47. 48. 64. 90. 91. 92. 95. 97. 98. 99. 124. 26. 116. 117. 17. 18. and then, no wonder if they be exceſſive, exceeding both the merit of the crime pretended, or the ability of the offender. How great a temptation is it to juſtice, to be ſevere, and ridgid in its ſentence, when the puniſhment of the offender is the inriching of them that paſſe the ſentence? (Nay, the judges themſelves are the grand offenders, and goe unpuniſhed), (p. 83. 84. 85.) and ſo it is here at Newcaſtle. (p. 87. (Q), p. 97. (C), p. 96. (H), p. 109. (D), p. 116.) One reaſon that induced ſome ſages of the law to affirme, that the latter kings of England, had diveſted themſelves of their power, to ſit perſonally in their courts of juſtice, and deligated it to, and inveſted the judges of the reſpective benches therewith, was, becauſe, in impoſing of fines, the king was both a judge, and party intereſted, not only as the fountain of juſtice, to be adminiſtered unto the people, but as the perſon into whoſe exchequers, and treaſury, the laws of England paid their fines. But the magiſtrates of Newcaſtle injoy thoſe privileges, which were thought unbeſeeming the kings of England. They are both judges, and parties.

They

They eftimate the offence, and receive the fine; and then how frequently covetoufneffe, and felf-intereft, fit on the bench, in the place of juftice, (p. 38.) the world may eafily judge; as appears in the cafe of Lewis Froft, and unjuft judge Bonner, hee having two-pence half-penny of all ballaft, and the other catchpole Bonner, to arreft the refufers.

Fourthly, Obftructing all indeavours for grant of a market at North Shields, fix miles from Newcaftle, and in another county, and 12 miles from any other market, in the fame county, and then robbing people of their commodities, in their own markets, and feizing on goods, carried through their town, alledging forraigne bought, and forraigne fold. Markets were for conveniences, and not for ingroffing all provifions, and peoples lives, (p. 92.) *Pag.* 75. 106. 107. 109. 111. 112. 113. 159. 168. 169.

Fifthly, For imprifoning poor artificers (p. 90. 91. 86.) for working in their own trades, at the town of Shields, though in another county, and detaining them, untill they enter into bond never to work there again, which is to engage themfelves, to abandon, and renounce that calling wherein they were brought up, to expofe themfelves, their wives, and children, to want, and beggary, or elfe to turn vagabons, (p. 183.) and defert the place of their habitations, being by thefe mens tyranny, neceffitated to leave their callings, or their dwellings. What fad fate hangs over the poor inhabitants of this town, to be deprived of the common privileges of englifhmen, fhall I fay? nay defpoyled of the common privileges of mankind, *In the fweat of their browes to eat their own bread, Genefis* 3. 19. and to yeild obedience to that precept of St. Paul, *Let him labour, working with his hands the thing that is good, that hee may have to give to him that needeth, Ephefians* 4. 28. Or that of the fame apoftle, 1. *Thef.* 4. 11. and 2. *Thef.* 3. 10. 11. 12. The character of Newcaftle, or rather indeed the ufurped power of the magiftrates there, fupercedes the commandments of God,

God. *Let every man*, faith St. Paul, *abide in the same calling wherein hee is called,* 1. Cor. 7. 20. If hee doth, fay the magiftrates of Newcaftle, he fhall not abide in Shields, nor in the neighbourhood of our corporation; as if they were a limbe of the beaft; fo that no man may work, (p. 77. 78. 168.) or buy, or fell, fave he that hath their mark, *Revel.* 13. 17. That is, unleffe hee be a member of that freedome, which ingroffeth fo much freedome to themfelves, that they leave no freedome at all to their poor neighbours. (p. 111.)

Sixthly, p. 74. 75. 82. (A), 90. 91. 79.) Imprifoning all that are not free of their corporation, that fhall indeavour to fave fhips in diftreffe, from perifhing in the river, and when they are funk, for want of help, feizing the goods of the mafters, and alfo imprifoning their perfons (78) many months. Let the world wherefoever it is moft favage, moft barbarous, fhew fuch an inftance of fuch an aggregation of injuftice, oppreffion, and cruelty as this; and (as wee fay, let them carry their coals) *If not to fave life bee to kill, and if not to doe good, when an opportunity is offered unto us, is to doe evill,* as, in our Saviours doctrine, certainly it is, *Mark* 3. 4. then not to fave a fhip, (p. 70.) I, and perhaps the mariners, and paffengers lives too, (77. 78.) when they have an opportunity, nay, when they are earneftly intreated, and their help implored, is in Gods accompt all one, as if they had funk the fhip, and drowned the men, (p. 86). Hee that doeth not prevent a mifchief, when it is in his power to doe it, is, in Gods accompt, the contriver, and the author of it; but that which is the great aggravation of their oppreffion, in this kind, and heighteneth it beyond any parallell is, they deny all help to fhips in diftreffe (p. 76. 77.) that fo making fhip wrack, (p. 19. 20. 74. 75. 76. 77. 78. 87. 79. 81. 90. 91.) That which in this is ufually alleged to take off from the horridneffe of their tyranny is, viz. that they muft fend

for

for help from Newcaftle, fignifies nothing; Newcaftle being feven miles from that harbour of Shields. *Whilft the graffe grows, the fteed ftarves*, as the proverb tells us; and while help is expected, the fhip is loft.

If thefe men could command the wind, and feas, not to rage, and fwell, but be hufhed into a calme, and the river kept from friezing (p. 63. 84. 85. 109. 112. 77. 78. 79. 80. 81. 82. 83,) untill they fent down help from Newcaftle, their reply might be admitted; but fince the wind, fea, and ice, are not controllable by their charter, what abominable tyranny, what favage inhumanity, is it to deny fhips in diftreffe, fuch help as is at hand, to preferve themfelves; cafes of neceffity make voyd proprieties, that which without the cafe of neceffity is theft, in the cafe of neceffity is not theft.

Men doe not defpife a thief, if hee fteale to fatisfy his foul when hee is hungry, Proverb. 6. 30. and the law faith, *when thou comeft into thy neighbours vineyard, thou maift eat grapes thy fill, at thine own pleafure, Deut. 23. 24*. In cafe of extreame neceffity, that all things are common, is the joynt opinion of all divines. This is the law of nature, and therefore not to be over-ruled, by any pofitive law, of any kingdome, or common-wealth; for in thefe cafes of extream neceffity, the perfon in this condition, taking that which is anothers, is not guilty of theft, for *Jure fuo utitur,* as the cafuifts determine, hee doth but make ufe of his own right; nor doth it come under the definition of theft, which is, *taking away that which is another mans, without his confent;* for as neceffity alters the property, and makes it his own, fo while he makes ufe of his own right, the other *tenetur confentire,* is bound to give his confent, and to acquiefce in the others injoyment of it. And therefore, in all pofitive laws, whereby property is diftinguifhed, there is none of them, which hold in cafe of extream neceffity; and fhall extream neceffity entitle a man to a part of another mans real poffeffion, by which there is *Damnum emergens*, fome damage, or diminution of the goods, and poffeffion of the owner, and yet free the invador from all imputation of injuftice, or ufurpation.

And fhall not a poor mafter of a fhip, in cafe of extream neceffity, (p. 77. 78. 76. 109. 79. 74. 80.) difpence with the privileges, and charter of Newcaftle, which at moft, can be but *lucrum ceffans*, a fufpenfion of their privileges, and gaine, and make ufe of fuch helps, for his prefervation, as Providence affords, without running the danger of fending for, and waiting the help from Newcaftle; without the ruine of thofe that fave him? Shall not extream neceffity, which is an apology for all the world, bee his juft apology, to plead his excufe in this cafe, and free him, and his helpers, from the tyranny, and perfecution of the magiftrates?

3. The prophet *Ifaiah*, tels us of fome magiftrates that were *companions of theeves, Ifaiah* 1. 23. *Ezekiel* tels us of others, that were *like evening wolves, ravening for their prey, Ezekiel* 22. 27. and *Zephany*, of others, that were like *roaring lyons, Zeph.* 3. 3. If any man doubt, whether thefe characters of oppreffive magiftrates, be applicable to thefe of Newcaftle, I fhall fay no more to them, than our Saviour did to Nathaniel in an other cafe, *Come and fee, Joh.* 1. 46.

Seventhly, Prohibiting gentlemen, and others, in the counties, both of Northumberland, and Durham, to fell their coales to fhips, to be tranfported to London, compelling all owners of colleries, to fell their coals to themfelves firft. If any fhall prefume to fell their coals, immediately to the fhips, without taking them in the way, they feize upon fuch coals, upon pretence that the owners of the coals are not free of their corporation, (pag. 21. 22. 100. 101. 98. 99. 102. 103. 104. 49. 84. 82. 81. 40. 193. 165. (D). And if this be not a monopoly, of as high

high a nature, and producing as ill effects, and those
of as large extent, as any, that (to the great content,
and satisfaction of the nation) hath been abolished,
let the * world judge. A welch pedigree, doth not
descend by more steps, and degrees, than the property of their coals is varied, while it is derived
from the owner of the collery, unto him that at last
buys the commodity, to spend it, as well trades as
others. The owners of colleries, must first sell the
coals to the magistrates of Newcastle, the magistrates
to the masters of ships, the master of ships to the
woodmongers, or wharfingers, and they to those
that spend them: Every change of the property ad-
ding to, and enhancing the price of the coals, thus
nterchangeably bought, and sold; which course, as
it picks some money out of the purses of every man,
that buys coals, besides bad * coals being thereby
vented, so it grinds the faces of the poor, who in
these latter years, by reason, mainly of this mono-
polizing of them, have found it as hard a matter to
fortify themselves against cold, as against hunger,
(p. 111.) whereas, if the owners of every collery
had free liberty, to sell (p. 124.) his coals to ships
immediately, Tinmouth haven, would afford two
hundred thousand chaldrons of coals in the year
more than now are vented, which would reduce the
late exorbitant excessive rates of coals, in the city of
London (p. 64. 65. 81.) to under twenty shillings a
chalder, all the year, winter as well as summer, and
bring into the common treasury above forty thousand
pounds per annum, (p. 60. 100. 101. 103.) Some
owners of coal-pits, will rather let their pits be fired,
like those at Benwell, and consume, than let their
coals to the magistrates of Newcastle. If the coal-
owners, in each county, from whence all coals come,
should be as refractory to the magistrates, in denying their coals, as the magistrates are to the masters,
(pag. 104. 99. 100. 98.) few, or none would be
brought to London, or any revenue raised.

* Which now as the case stands, the city is cheated in buying of slates as well as coals. p. 50.

Eighthly,

Eighthly, Forcing all ſhips, up the river ſix miles, amongſt dangerous ſands, ſhelves, and the bulks of ſunk ſhips, (p. 74. 75. 76. 77. 78. 84. 99. 100.) that ſo they may caſt out their ballaſt, upon their ſhoars, and all for the greedineſs of receiving eight-pence, for every tun of ballaſt, which hath occaſioned the ſpoyl, and loſs of many ſhips, to the utter undoing of the maſters, and owners of the ſhips, and the deſtruction of the lives of many poor ſeamen, and mariners, whoſe blood will be required at their hands, who put them on thoſe dangers, in which they periſhed, beſides their choaking up the moſt part of that river, by forcing the ballaſt up their ſandy hils, near the ſaid town of Newcaſtle, many thouſand tuns whereof is blown, and waſhed down into that river, (p. 83. 84). They will neither preſerve the river, nor let doctor Swinbourn, vice admiral for the county of Durham, doe it, who hath fined ſome of the magiſtrates hundreds of pounds, for damages, &c.

Laſtly, Countenancing their officers in their oppreſſions, nay, in their very murthers, as in the caſe of Thomas Rutter, with others, who having forfeited their lives to juſtice, for killing Ann, the wife of Thomas Cliff, of North Shields, was, by their power, and favor, reſcued from that death; which they juſtly deſerved, (p. 86). God would not ſuffer his altar to be a ſanctuary to a wilful murtherer, neither would king John, their patron, (p. 38). *If a man come preſumptuouſly upon his neighbor, to ſlay him, thou ſhalt take him from mine altar, that he may die*, Exo. 21. 14. The law of England defines what murther is, (p. 168). *Blood defileth the land, and the land cannot be cleanſed of the blood that is ſhed therein, but by the blood of him that ſhed it,* Numb. 35. 33. When therefore God ſhall make inquiſition, they *that ſtaid him, that offered violence to the blood of his neighbor, and ſhould have gone to the pit*, Prov. 20. 17. will be found to communicate in this

this murder, and involved in the fame guilt, with him that committed it, but the good God be merciful to them, that have not approved, or confented to this wickednefs; For *though our eyes did fee this blood, yet our hands did not fhed it*; and therefore let every one that would wafh his hands clean, from that blood, pray, as God prefcribed, *Be merciful, O Lord, unto thy people Ifrael, whom thou haft redeemed, and lay not innocent blood unto thy people Ifraels charge,* Deut. 21. 7. 8.

Thus have I given you a fhort view of the tyrannical oppreffive practices of the magiftrates of Newcaftle, whofe fin receives no fmall aggravation from their office, and calling, in that they are magiftrates, whom God hath furnifhed with authority, to that end, that they might prevent, and redrefs injuries, done by others, and *execute wrath upon evill doers,* Rom. 13. 4. So that in their oppreffions, they fin againft the very end of their calling, they transform the very image of Gods power, and juftice, which they fuftain, into the image of Gods enemy, Satan, whom herein they refemble, and become, after a fort, wickedneffes in high places, as the devils are; for amongft them, as much as any where, is that of Solomon verified, *I faw under the fun, the place of judgement, that wickednefs was there, and the place of righteoufnefs, that iniquity was there,* Ecclef. 3. 16. And although attempts hitherto, and all indeavors, for redrefs of thefe oppreffive courfes, have proved abortive, and fruitlefs, no man compaffionating the people with Saul, fo much as to afke, *What ayleth this people, that they weep,* 1. Sam. 11. 5. No, after many addreffes, petitions, remonftrances, and futes at law, being ftifled by the inftigation of corrupt perfons, then in power, and obftructed, by the mutability, and changes, we have too juft reafon to complain with Solomon, *Behold the tears of fuch as were oppreffed, and they had no comforters, and on the fides of their oppreffors there was power, but they, the oppreffed oppreſſed, had no comforter, Eccleſ.* 4. 1. Yet at this time we are not without good hopes, but that the cries of the poor, and the oppreſſed, will enter into the ears, and hearts of this preſent power, That they will be as a *hiding place from the winde, and a covert from the tempeſt, as rivers of water in a dry place, as the ſhadow of a great rock in a weary land, Iſa.* 32. 2.

But if our hopes now fail us, we muſt ſit down, and ſigh out that of Solomon, *If thou ſeeſt the oppreſſion of the poor, and violent perverting of judgment and juſtice in a province, marvail not at the matter, for Hee that is higher than the higheſt regardeth, and there be higher than they, Eccles.* 5. 8.

THE

THE TABLE.

A

	Page
ATCHESON	91
Arresting in others names	181
Arresting out of a liberty	157
Arresting by false writs	183
Attorney	134, 185
Admiralty river	16, 18, 50, 122
Aldermen	23, 24, 139
Articles for the river	39 to 45
Army at battell	125
Army men disarmed	164
Artificers	168, 169, 90, 91
Acton Burnel	29
Andronicus	74
Attaint against a jury	154
Ad quod damnum	159
Act for free trade	121, 173
Alehouses	190

B

Bounders of Newcastle	8, 9, 10, 11, 12, 18
Bigs	82
Bowes	91
Bonner	55, 79, 90
Beets	76
Buckingham	16
Bishop and justice	39
Bribery	10
Ballast, 43, 44, 47, 48, 80, 83, 85, 92, 95, 109, 110, 122, 123, 155, 80, 98, 99, 100, 50, 51, 52, 57, 59, 85, 101.	
Bonds	47, 91, 109
Bayl denied	88, 95, 156, 145
Bread and water fed	89
Bread nor beer at Shields	109, 61, 113, 123
Beasts blood	111
Blewet	108
Bidleston	117

E e   Burgess.

	Page
Burgesses	31, 138
Bayliffs oath	135
Belman	114
Barrator	165
Butler	98
Bradford	92
Bracton	90

C

Charters, 7, 8, 10, 11, 12, 14, 18, 21, 33, 55, 56, 116, 124, 125, 126, 157, 159, 133, 174, 49.
Corporation — 120, 172
Coroner — 19, 24, 25, 75, 107, 148, 160
Customs on coals, 104, 105, 28, 55, 56, 81, 100, 101, 102, 103, 104, 105.
Court — 24
Conservators peace — 25
And river — 40
Commissioners river — 46, 122, 40
Combination — 78, 99
Coals, 104, 9, 49, 28, 193, 124, 63, 84, 98, 99, 100, 101, 123, 55, 56, 184, 143, 9, 10, 11, 12, 13, 14, 15, 17, 102, 188, 21, 25, 33, 76, 77.
Conspiracies in art — 168
Cartwright — 100
Cudworth — 102, 103
Customers — 144, 176
Twelve companies — 21
Councils names — 44, 46, 52, 58
Crosier — 51
Cliffs trial — 61, 79, 82, 86, 87
Committee — 65
Carpenters — 90, 91
Castle of Darrel — 48
Commission sewers — 153
Condemned by law — 141
Confiscations — 124, 112, 31, 71, 106, 109
Corn — 108, 111
Cason — 81, 77

D

Dudley and Empson — 38
Drowning — 63, 75, 107, 109
Dogs and cats eaten — 111, 127
Debts — 29
Duties on coals — 104, 105

Distress

	Page
Diftrefs	160
Damage to fhips	80, 81
Drunkennefs	37, 117, 190
Deanes claim	125
Duke Venice	176
Dawfon	102, 103, 104, 107
Darrel	48

E

K. Edw 1.	156
Edw. 2.	161
Edw. 3.	164
Edw. 6.	168
Q. Elizab.	13, 14, 15, 21, 179
Extortion	121, 131, 157, 182
Evidence	135, 116
Expofitions	130
Executions	182

F

Fleta	90
Foreftallers	19, 170, 180, 110, 111
Fines,	17, 20, 25, 35, 64, 90, 92, 95, 97, 98, 99, 124, 167
Fifhermen	48
Felons	25, 26, 116, 163
Fees by corporation	152
Fenwick	145, 146
Farrow	110
Fee-farm	7, 11, 12
Fifh royal	20

G

Gates lockt	43
Grounds fenced	43, 44, 82, 83, 118, 119
Gardiners	62, 63, 67, 110
Goods	64, 123
Grenaway	113
Gatefhead	172, 178
Gold and filver	166
Green	97
Grievances to be redreffed	167
Gallows	21, 26
Gaolers	164
Grammer-fchool	32
Governor	33, 34

E e 2   Government

					Page
Government	—	—	—	—	37
Gofnal	—	—	—	—	77

H

K. Hen. 3. charter	—	—	—		8
Hoaft-mens charter	—	—	14, 28, 32, 49, 55,	99
Horth	—	—	—	56,	83
K. Hen. 4.	—	—	—	—	13
L. Howard	—	—	—	—	16
Sir Heath	—	—	—	50, 51,	118
Hilton	—	—	—	57,	109
Hanging	—	—	—	26,	114
Heads cut off	—	—	—	—	127
Heathens practice	—	—	—		93
Hume	—	—	—	75,	107
Sir Haflerigge	—	—	106, 108,	113
Hefilwood	—	—	78, 85,	92
Harrifon	—	—	—	86,	93
Hall	—	—	—	—	91
Habeas corpus	—	—	—		89
Hornes Mirror	—	—	—		90
K Herrolds battle	—	—	—		125
K. Hen. 3.	—	—	—		141
K. Hen. 4.	—	—	—		142
K. Hen. 5.	—	—	—		143
K. Hen. 6.	—	—	—		144
K. Hen. 7.	—	—	—		148
K. Hen. 8.	—	—	—		151

I

K. John	—	—	—	1, 7, 137, 38
K James	—	—	—	38
Indictments	—	—	—	87, 188, 147
Imprifoning	—	—	17, 35, 82, 88, 89, 90, 91
Juftices	—	18, 20, 24, 25, 116, 142, 164, 165
Judges and jurors	—	19, 96, 109, 116, 154, 155, 172
Ingroffers	—	—	19, 107, 110, 111, 112, 170
Jarrow	—	—	—	53, 81, 96, 119
Jury	—	—	—	135, 154
Information of penal ftatutes	—	—	188, 171, 172

K

Keelesmen	—	—	—	43, 105, 143
Katherines liberties	—	—	—	46
Kents land	—	—	—	125

Keeble

	Page
Keeble	81
Kings oath	126, 136, 137

I.

Limitation of actions	189
Laws, 7, 34, 36, 37, 88, 96, 116, 117, 125, 126, 130, 141, 17, 22, 23.	
Liberties forfeited	45, 46, 124, 172
Lamb	160
Leafe grand collery	26
Lever	99, 100
Low	80
Lyme	82
Lambert	91
Lyng	95
Lumfdall	106
Lands purchafe	177, 17, 11, 33
Letters counterfeited	83

M

Morpeth burnt	4
Mayor chofen, 22, 23, 24, 25, 38, 39, 119, 120, 167, 137	
Mortmain	26, 177
Murder	38, 87, 185, 168
Markets, 22, 29, 63, 75, 106, 107, 108, 109, 112, 113, 124, 159, 169.	
Merchants	124
Mariners	29
Mallen	76, 80
Morfs	81
Midford	82
Mirriton	103
Meafures, coals	84
Miferies	126
Q. Mary	178

N

Newcaftle, 16, 21, 66, 67, 71, 72, 118, 121, 122, 143, 128	
Northumberland	126, 127, 128, 129
Navigation	121
Normans	125

O

Oliver, lord protector	121
Officers	

		Page
Officers	19, 23, 24, 29, 33, 38, 87, 157,	167
Outlawed		23, 24

Oath, 23, 38, 42, 78, 92, 93, 94, 95, 97, 126, 134, 135, 136, 137, 138, 139, 168.

Ordinances	—	—	149, 193, 194
Ordes wife	—	—	106
Objections	—	—	118

P

Parliament	—	—	5, 59, 62, 193
Punishments	—	—	17, 47, 62
Petition right	—	—	191
Pleading	—	—	33, 29, 66, 72
Penalties	—	—	35, 25
Profits	—	—	36
Purse cutting	—	—	92, 182

Prisons, 25, 64, 77, 88, 89, 90, 91, 92, 93, 95, 99, 161

Peach	—	—	97
Prisoners	—	—	164, 90
Pots	—	—	80
Pilots	—	—	123
Phillips	—	—	79, 84, 104
Perjury	—	79, 82, 92, 93,	179
Pye	—	—	98
Poor	—	—	183
Provision	63, 101, 109, 110, 111, 112,	113
Prentice	—	117, 118,	179
Pardon	—	—	31
Prerogative	—	—	125
Pope	—	—	137

Q

| Quo warranto | — | — | 31, 37, 120, 159 |

R

K. Rich. 2.	—	—	12, 173
Ryots	—	—	177, 88, 144
Regrators	—	—	19, 170
Rates	—	86, 106, 107,	166
Robbing	—	—	169
Recorder	—	—	23, 24
Recognizans	—	—	29

River, 84, 109, 111, 112, 38, 46, 62, 63, 99, 100, 152, 153, 155, 53, 59, 64, 65, 80, 82, 84, 109, 118.

| Rewards | — | — | 47 |

Read

THE TABLE.

	Page
Read — — — —	102, 98,
Reavely — — — —	108
Revenue — — —	81, 100, 101
Readhead — — — —	90
Rawling — — — —	99
Rebels — — — —	29

S

Sheriff —	13, 25, 142, 145, 147, 156, 162, 182, 183
Sueing — — —	17, 49, 98, 106, 108
Seele — — —	17, 30, 34, 165
Sparhawke — — —	18, 151
School — — — —	32
Steward — — —	33
Servants — — —	110

Ships unload, 35, 43, 44, 60, 64, 123, 124, 111, 112, 75, 76, 77, 78, 79, 80, 81, 82, 86, 98, 109, 123, 111, 108.

Star chamber — —	49, 93, 191
Ship-carpenters — —	123, 61
Strafford — — —	38
Sands patent — — —	56
Spanish inquisition — — —	93
Straw-mat — — —	97
Seamen custome-free — —	112
Symonds — — —	112
Scoulds — — —	117
Stock commonwealth — —	121
Salt works — — —	123
Scots burning people — —	128
Salkeild — — — —	88
Sergeants — — — —	114
Stabbing — — — —	184
Survey — — — —	195

T

Talbot — — — —	98
Toule —	30, 101, 107, 109, 111, 152, 157
Trades —	21, 58, 84, 118, 121, 170, 173, 176
Tyrants law — — —	74
Tye — — — —	77
Tickets — — — —	47
Taylor — — —	90, 111
Trinity-house, London — —	118
Tyn — — — —	101
Tobacco — — — —	106

Thorp,

Thorp, judge	106
Table of fees	152
Tax only by parliament	159
Tempeſt patent	55

V

Victuals	75, 112, 166, 168, 31
Voyages loſt	80, 81, 99, 100, 101, 104, 111
Voyages gained	81, 86, 100, 105
Uſher	32
Uſurped power pardoned	31

W

Wall	10
Wreck	19, 20, 74, 75, 76, 77, 78, 79, 162
Workmen	183, 90, 91
Wages	86, 78
Watching	47, 110
Willy	81
Witch-finder	116
Wheeler	114
Wyard	97
Warrants	110, 88, 104, 159, 160
William conqueror	125, 126
Water	109, 110
Weſt	113
Williamſon	106
Weights and meaſures	109

Y

Yaxley	81
Yelverton	49

F I N I S.

www.ingramcontent.com/pod-product-compliance
Lightning Source LLC
Chambersburg PA
CBHW032134230426
43672CB00011B/2330